Scared Silly

Scared Silly

25 Tales to Tickle and Thrill

Dianne de Las Casas

Illustrated by Soleil Lisette

A Teacher Ideas Press Book

Libraries Unlimited
An Imprint of ABC-CLIO, LLC

A B C ⬇ C L I O

Santa Barbara, California • Denver, Colorado • Oxford, England

Library of Congress Cataloging-in-Publication Data

De Las Casas, Dianne.
  Scared silly : 25 tales to tickle and thrill / Dianne de Las Casas ; Illustrated by Soleil Lisette.
    p. cm.
  "A Teacher Ideas Press book."
  Includes bibliographical references and index.
  ISBN 978-1-59158-732-3 (pbk : alk. paper) 1. Supernatural. 2. Horror tales 3. Storytelling. I. Lisette, Soleil. II. Title.
  GR500.D43 2009
  808.8'037—dc22   2009026363

13 12 11 10 9   1 2 3 4 5

This book is also available on the World Wide Web as an eBook.
Visit www.abc-clio.com for details.

ABC-CLIO, LLC
130 Cremona Drive, P.O. Box 1911
Santa Barbara, California 93116-1911

This book is printed on acid-free paper ∞
Manufactured in the United States of America

For Karleen Good,
My Junior High English teacher,
who inspired and encouraged me
and who still does, to this day!
Dianne de Las Casas

For Eliana,
My little sister with a big heart.
I love you, "Silly-ana!"
Soleil Lisette

Contents

The Scary Stories

Introduction

There's nothing like the thrill of a good ghost story! I've been telling scary stories for a long time. It started in elementary school. I loved giving my younger brother the heebie-jeebies by telling him a good ghostly tale. I'd lie in his room in the top bunk while he was in the bottom bunk. I'd tell him stories about the monster that lived underneath the bed. Inevitably, he would climb into the top bunk, and I would leave! (For those of you wondering, my brother has since gotten back at me many times over. He now scares me!) Then there were the Scouts. As a Scout, you learned the art of spooky telling when you went camping with your troupe. Many of the stories I tell today are from my childhood.

Scared Silly: 25 Tales to Tickle and Thrill was inspired by my spooky story program of the same title, "Scared Silly." Requests for "Scared Silly" run year-round, not just during Halloween.

Children love a good spooky story. It's like a roller-coaster ride—the thrill of the chill. Yet at the end of the ride, the children know they are safe. I have written this book as a "primer" on telling scary stories. In addition, there are 25 spooky tales. Many are storytellers' classics. Each story is annotated with suggestions on how to tell the tale. I have also rated the stories using a "Spook-O-Meter" so you can determine the age and grade appropriateness of each story.

So grab a flashlight, and let's get "scared silly!"

Warmly,

Dianne de Las Casas
dianne@storyconnection.net
www.storyconnection.net

Why Tell a Scary Story?

Telling a scary story is a fine line to walk. Many audience members, particularly elementary and middle school aged children, will beg for scary stories, but when you tell them, you may hear protests from angry parents. In his Web article "What's Scary Enough?" (www.oddsbodkin.com/articles/What%27s_Scary_Enough.html), celebrated storyteller and musician Odds Bodkin suggests: "Kids only rejoice in scariness when deep down they feel safe and know it's not real. Scariness tickles a safe child in a fun way, but it deepens real fears in an unsafe child. So know who's in your audience. Offer the option for those who would rather not listen to leave."

The key is to know your child. Some souls find scary stories disturbing, even at mature ages. The question arises whether dwelling in this sensitivity to things macabre too long—rather than coming to terms with life's scariness early—is good or not. But that's a decision only you can make.

—Odds Bodkin, professional storyteller and author

Richard Young and Judy Dockery Young, authors of *The Scary Story Reader* (August House, 1993) and *Favorite Scary Stories of American Children* (August House, 1990), say: "Children love scary stories and, in fact, benefit from them by facing and mastering the little moments of 'fear for fun' these tales provide. Naturally, every storyteller needs to know the audience and judge the appropriateness of every frightening folktale."

With every story comes responsibility. You are responsible for the stories you share. Don't neglect your responsibility. Sometimes a story that has grotesque and senseless violence is not one to share with others. Don't choose your stories like a shopping list; choose like it will affect someone, because it will. You determine the outcome by not only your telling, but your story choice.
—Kevin Cordi, professional storyteller

In the introduction to *Haunted Bayou and Other Cajun Ghost Stories* (August House, 1994), the late J. J. Reneaux stated: "The ghost stories in this collection have been passed down from generation to generation through storytelling. They have served not only as entertainment but as teaching tools, helping tellers and listeners remember the legends, myths, and history of their people. They have also acted as warnings, cautioning against the dangers of breaking rules and taboos of society. Now as then, tales of ghosts provide comfort by allowing people to face their worst fears without true danger."

Diane Ladley, who is known as "America's Ghost Storyteller," explains the dynamics of fear and says that the brain's using fear as a means of signaling danger is a way to maximize the chances of survival in a dangerous situation. Diane says scary stories

- provide a safe way to exercise and develop our fear system;
- teach appropriate actions and options to choose from;
- Desensitize us to scary things to help us cope—habituation; and
- Sensitize us to real-life fearful situations and build caution. (personal communication)

Kids need make-believe violence to help them cope with real-life dangers.
—Diane Ladley, "America's Ghost Storyteller"

Roberta Simpson Brown, author of *Queen of the Cold-Blooded Tales* (August House, 1993), offers this explanation of why she believes stories have value: "When I became a professional storyteller, I realized that one thing all human beings have in common is the powerful emotion of fear. I saw that scary stories grabbed the attention of the most reluctant listener. When I look out at the huge audiences that come to hear ghost tales, I am convinced that people have a need to share fear and realize that they are not alone."

Telling stories is something people have done for thousands of years, for most of us like being scared in that way. Since there isn't any danger, we think it is fun.
—Alvin Schwartz, *Scary Stories to Tell in the Dark* (HarperCollins, 1981)

Fear is one of the world's most universal emotions. Every culture has ghost stories. The value of telling a scary story becomes apparent when you see a group of children beg for more spooky stories after you've just finished telling a ghostly tale. When children realize that other children share their trepidation, the story audience becomes a safe place within which to process their fears.

How to Tell a Scary Story: Various "Scarious"

It is important to know the various types of scary stories. Familiarizing yourself with these will enable you to build a larger repertoire of stories suitable for all age ranges.

Jump Tales

Jump tales are usually told with a "gotcha!" at the end, a surprise ending intended to make audiences jump. They are great for older elementary kids, for sharing around a campfire, or at a sleepover. Examples of jump tales are "Taily Po," and "A Dark, Dark Story." The late, great Jackie Torrence said, "But when you tell a Jump Tale, remember that the expressions in your face and your gestures are what children watch, but your whole body is telling the story. You must put all of yourself into it" (*Jackie Tales*, Avon, 1998).

Legends

Legends are born out of actual events. The stories eventually become so big and exaggerated that they turn into legends. An example is "The Legend of Sleepy Hollow."

Urban Legends

American kids love urban legends, stories that originated in or around urban or city areas. Urban legend origins are usually difficult to trace. People claim that an urban legend is "absolutely true" because they heard it from a friend or another reliable source. A good example of an urban legend is "The Hitchhiker." Urban legends are great for older audiences such as teenagers.

Ghost Stories

Ghost stories are those tales of the supernatural in which ghosts are sighted or play a major role. Some are about hauntings in which spirits are said to roam the earth. Others truly send chills up the spine. Many people claim that their ghost stories really happened. A great example is the stories from the Myrtles Plantation in St. Francisville, Louisiana (purported to be one of America's most haunted houses).

The Gory Story

Gory stories are what I consider "slice and dice" horror and not at all appropriate for early childhood and elementary aged children. They are full of gratuitous violence and are often the fodder of teen horror flicks.

Slightly Spooky

Slightly spooky tales are designed with a younger audience in mind. They draw out the suspense and spookiness until the end, when the storyteller delivers a funny punch line. Many of these stories began as jokes. They are also referred to as "shaggy dog" stories. Good examples are "Rap, Rap, Rap," "The Viper," and "The Coffin."

How to Determine the Age Appropriateness of Your Story Selection

How old should a child be to listen to a scary story? First, the answer depends on your definition of "scary." Second, age appropriateness is very subjective and dependent on the child's maturity level. Finally, it depends on the "permissions" of your audience, the types of scary stories they are *expecting* to hear.

That being said, I like to follow some general guidelines when telling stories. If you are billing your scary storytelling program as a "family program," then it should be age appropriate for the youngest audience member. You have to deliver stories that work well with all ages.

Pre-K and K (Ages 3–5)

At this age, children are often easily frightened and have a low tolerance for fear. Many children at this age are afraid of Santa Claus and the Easter Bunny. Stories told to this audience should be short, silly, fun, and participatory. Characters should be exaggerated and cartoony.

Grades 1–3 (Ages 6–8)

Children at this age have developed a greater fear of the unknown. They are afraid of the dark, invisible monsters in the closet, creatures under the bed, and things that go bump in the night. They are also likely to jump into bed with their parents if they are truly frightened. Scary stories for this age group should be suspenseful, silly, animated, and slightly spooky. "Shaggy dog" tales and jump stories work well with this group.

Grades 4–6 (Ages 9–12)

These children are testing their boundaries and limitations. They are often heavily influenced by their peers. They are no longer "babies" and purport to "not be afraid of anything." They want their friends to think they are "cool." Don't let their brave facades fool you; they still get scared! These children purposely choose scary story books because they enjoy the thrill of the adrenaline rush. With this age group, you can venture into more complex stories with intricate plot twists, psychological thrills, and scariness. Suspenseful stories with lots of creepy sound effects and jump tales work well. Though these children are older, it is important to assuage their fears at the end of the storytelling session, letting them know that they are safe.

Grades 7–12 (Ages 13–18)

Kids at this age love to be truly frightened. These are the young adults who play "truth or dare," often asking for the "dare." They enjoy "true" ghost stories, gory stories, and those that deliver a psychological "high speed chase." They like white-knuckle, edge-of-your-seat terror. Good examples of classic stories for this age group are "The Monkey's Paw" and "The Tell-Tale Heart."

Establishing an Environment of Trust

Fear is a funny thing. For children, an environment of "shared fear" such as a roller-coaster ride, a frightening movie, or a scary storytelling session can actually act as a bonding agent and help build an environment of trust. Children will huddle together, hold hands, and cover each other's eyes and ears, even when they don't know each other!

But you have to be very careful. As the storyteller, you hold all the power in your voice, your face, and your body. One wrong turn can send your audience careening down Chaos Chasm. It is your responsibility to give your audience a thrill ride yet return them safely to the ground.

You can establish trust with your audience through your body language. Smiling and open body language draws people in. Animated, cartoonlike characters appeal to smaller children. Large gestures, loud voices, frightening faces, and "Hulk-like" body movement causes audiences to shrink away. Know when to be bold and when to pull back. Carefully watch your audience's reaction. Intense fear and anxiety will cause tears, widened eyes, dilated pupils, shallow or rapid breathing, and closed body language such as covering the eyes and sticking fingers in the ears.

Storytelling with Pacing, Timing, Pitch, and Tone

Telling spooky tales is all about pacing, timing, pitch, and tone (PTPT). These are a storyteller's secret weapons. Learn how to master PTPT, and you will be able to control your audience's reaction when telling tales that tickle and thrill.

Pacing

Pacing is how fast or slow the story moves when you tell it. If a boy is running away from something through the woods, the pacing of your voice (your words) should be fast to indicate urgency. On the other hand, if the boy is tiptoeing to peek inside a house, your voice should move at a slower pace to indicate creeping and sneaking. Pacing a story just right, so that it is told neither too fast nor too slow, is vital in keeping your audience's attention.

Timing

Timing in a story is very important. It allows your listeners to process what they are hearing. It also allows the storyteller to deliver lines effectively, creating tension, drama, suspense, and relief. In the story "The Viper," the last line depends entirely on timing. When it is delivered properly, the entire audience erupts in simultaneous laughter. Silence or a dramatic pause can add more suspense and tension in a story than trying to fill the space with words. Saying, "It was just the wind . . . [BIG PAUSE] or was it?" allows readers to ponder that question. To get a sense of timing, listen to a joke with a good punch line. How the punch line is delivered depends on the comedian's sense of timing.

Pitch

The pitch of your voice is the highs and lows of your vocal notes. You can carry your listeners on a rising crest or set them down gently in a falling tide. Your pitch can be as bold as a thunder bolt or as timid as a light drizzle. You can create characters in a story through your pitch. A high-pitched voice could be that of a mouse; a low-pitched voice could be that of a lion.

Tone

In this context, tone refers both to the tone of your voice and that of your story. Your story's overall tone has the power to influence your audience. A story such as "Going on a Ghost Hunt" will need a cartoony, comic tone, because it is meant for a young audience, whereas a story such as "The Hitchhiker" can begin in a more ominous tone, foreshadowing its suspense and tension.

Thirteen Tips for Telling Spooky Stories

1. Know Your Audience

If you are telling to a mixed age group, stories should be appropriate for the youngest member of your audience, unless the program has been advertised otherwise. Select stories that are appropriate for the age group to whom you are telling. A too-scary story can result in disaster. A story that is too "babyish" for an older crowd will cause your audience to lose interest.

2. Adjust Your Space

If you are telling to a mixed group, arrange the seating so that smaller children are with older siblings, parents, or grandparents. Seating the children in a close cluster makes for a more ambient telling, and children feel safer when they are in a group. If appropriate, dim the lights.

3. Permission to Leave

Give audience members permission to leave if they find the story too spooky. Sometimes children will sit through a torturous storytelling session because they do not know it is okay to leave. It is nice to have an alternate space for these children—an area where they can play or color.

4. Spooky or Scary?

Know the difference! Children need to know what they are getting when it comes to spooky stories. Are you telling spine-tingling tales or super scary stories? Let your audience know so that they have the option to leave.

5. Comforting Ritual

Sometimes a comforting or silly ritual can help assuage children's fears. For instance, you can say to the children, "If you get too scared later, do this [*Show children a raspberry with your mouth and have them repeat it.*] and say: 'I'm not afraid'!" [*Wildly wave a pointer finger side to side.*]

6. The Tale's Title

Feel free to adapt stories to suit your personal storytelling style. That's what storytellers do. When choosing a title for your tale, create one that does not give the story away. For example, I changed "The Nail in the Attic" to "The Attic" because the words "The Nail" gave away the punch line of the story.

7. Audience Participation

Audience participation makes a scary story not so scary because the children also become the tellers of the tale. It gives them ownership of the story, and ownership is power. It also provides a distraction from the terror their imaginations can invoke. Try telling "Tilly and the Heebie-Jeebie Man" without audience participation, and you will see a completely different audience. It can be a downright terrifying tale. On the other hand, adding a participatory refrain allows children a break from their natural tendency to turn simple fear into terror.

8. Sound Effects

Sound effects can be a very effective device in adding a spooky ambience to a tale. Great sound effects for scary stories include howling winds, creaking doors, footsteps, scratching, growling, knocking, thumping, and other loud, creepy noises. If you invite the children to participate in the spooky sound effects (this is great for younger children), it becomes less scary for them.

9. The Bell Curve

When putting a scary story program together for a mixed age group, generally follow a bell curve. Warm up with a not-so-scary story, gradually increasing the intensity of the suspense and thrill. Reach the peak with a spine-tingling, hair-raising tale and then decrease the intensity by ending with a funny spooky story, joke, or song. Remember to announce to your audience that your stories will be increasing in intensity, so that people have the option to leave if they wish.

From *Scared Silly: 25 Tales to Tickle and Thrill* by Dianne de Las Casas. Illustrated by Soleil Lisette. Santa Barbara, CA: Libraries Unlimited/Teacher Ideas Press. Copyright © 2010.

10. Suspense and Relief

For children, listening to a scary story is about suspense and relief. Build the suspense in your stories, creating tension and drama, but be sure to provide a vehicle for release and relief. Children, especially, need to know that they are okay at the end of a scary story.

11. Voice, Face, and Body

The use of your voice, face, and body is essential in telling scary stories. They all work together to persuade and influence your audience. Don't be afraid to exaggerate expressions and add vocal variety when telling to children. Use your body to create characters and denote scene changes. Consistently block your space. If you have an imaginary table on your right-hand side, it should remain on that side.

12. Audience's Reaction

Gauge your listeners' reaction when telling your stories. Be prepared to scale back your telling if they show an undue amount of fear or anxiety. External signs of distress include tears, widened eyes, dilated pupils, shallow or rapid breathing, and closed body language (covering eyes or plugging ears).

13. Bringing the Audience Home Safe

As storytellers, it is our responsibility to make sure our audience is safe, especially when it consists of children. End a program with a funny story, joke, song, silly antic, or chant, such as, "Give yourselves a big pat on the back. Our tales are done, and that is that."

The Scary Stories

The Spook-O-Meter

The Spook-O-Meter graphic throughout the book is designed to help you gauge the appropriateness of each story for your audience. When telling scary stories, you can always tell "up" but not "down." That means that stories appropriate for younger audiences can be told to older audiences; however, stories for older audiences are not usually appropriate for younger audiences. There are times when I allow you to make adjustments to the story to change its "Spook-O-Meter" factor. Stories in the Spook-O-Meter 2 range are the best ones to tell to a multi-aged audience such as mixed grade levels and family audiences.

Fun and silly. Stories are appropriate for ages 3–5 or grades pre-K–K.

Slightly spooky, humorous, and suspenseful. Stories are appropriate for ages 6–8 or grades 1–3. These stories work for a family audience as well because of the humor.

Spooky and spine-tingling. Stories are appropriate for ages 9–10 or grades 4–5.

Super spooky and bone-chilling. Stories are appropriate for ages 11–13 or middle school.

Super duper spooky. Stories are appropriate for the bravest of souls.

A Dark, Dark Story

Note from Dianne: This is a great story to tell to younger children. It's short, but the intensity and quietness of your voice can make the story suspenseful and spooky. There is a great jump at the end. If telling to the very young (grades pre-K or K), scale back the jump at the end so that you don't scare the children to death (no pun intended).

It was a dark, dark night. [*Cover your eyes with your hands and then pull them apart slowly, with peering eyes.*]

In that dark, dark night, there was a white full moon. [*Arch your arms over your head in a circle to symbolize the moon.*]

That white full moon hung over a dark, dark forest. [*Raise your hands slowly, straight up over your head, while wiggling your fingers to symbolize the forest.*]

In that dark, dark forest, there was a dark, dark house. [*With both arms, form an upside down "V" over your head to symbolize a house.*]

In that dark, dark house, there was a dark, dark room. [*Tiptoe as though you are entering a room.*]

In that dark, dark room, there was a dark, dark closet. [*Mime as though you are opening a closet door.*]

From *Scared Silly: 25 Tales to Tickle and Thrill* by Dianne de Las Casas. Illustrated by Soleil Lisette. Santa Barbara, CA: Libraries Unlimited/Teacher Ideas Press. Copyright © 2010.

In that dark, dark closet, there was a dark, dark chest. [*Form an imaginary "chest" with your arms in front of your chest.*]

In that dark, dark chest, there was a dark, dark box. [*With one hand, draw a square in the air to symbolize the box.*]

In that dark, dark box there was a . . . [*Lower your voice while saying "In that dark, dark box there was a . . . ." Make a creaking noise and motion as though you are opening a hinged box.*]

Chocolate bar! [*Say "chocolate bar" very loudly for the jump effect. If you want to give the ending a humorous release, mime as though you are opening the chocolate bar and bite into it, exaggerating the loud chewing. Then offer the "chocolate bar" to a teacher or grown-up, asking, "Do you want some?" Wipe the chocolate off your face and then wipe your hands on the grown-up's sleeve. You will hear a lot of "ewwwws" and laughter.*]

The Attic

Note from Dianne: This is a jump tale that is less intense, mostly suspense. It's a "shaggy dog" and a groaner, perfect to relieve the tension or to warm up a group for scarier stories. It's a great story to tell in the first person. Tell it as though it actually happened to you. This gives the story a great deal of believability.

When I was young, there was a strange old man [*Punctuate "strange old man."*] who lived in our neighborhood. We all called him "Mr. Jake." Well, Mr. Jake had a dog named "King." Why Mr. Jake called him "King," I don't know. He was a mangy old mutt with matted fur. One of his ears was longer than the other, and King walked with a limp. But Mr. Jake loved that dog, yes he did! [*Punctuate "yes he did!"*] I think King was Mr. Jake's only true friend.

Every day, at the same time, Mr. Jake got up and walked around the neighborhood with King. I know this because as I stood and waited for the school bus to pick me up every morning, Mr. Jake and King walked by. Now, Mr. Jake never acknowledged my presence, but King always tilted his head and seemed to grin at me, his tongue lolling to the side.

One morning, I was standing at the bus stop when Mr. Jake walked by . . . [*pause*] WITHOUT King! From the look on Mr. Jake's face, I knew something was wrong. I asked, "Mr. Jake, where's King?"

Mr. Jake gave me a one-word answer [*big pause*]: "Missing."

I'll never forget the next few days. All hours of the day and night, Mr. Jake walked. He screamed for King until his voice disappeared. Some say that after that, Mr. Jake never opened his mouth again. [*Say this in a hushed tone.*]

Then one day, Mr. Jake was inside his house. He heard noises coming from inside his attic.

Shuffle. Shuffle. Drag. Shuffle. Shuffle. Drag . . .

He grabbed his gun and took off his boots and his socks. He didn't want to give whatever was in his attic warning that he was coming.

Slowly, Mr. Jake climbed the attic stairs. [*Mime climbing.*]

Again, he heard the noises coming from inside the attic.

Shuffle. Shuffle. Drag. Shuffle. Shuffle. Drag . . .

Mr. Jake reached the attic door. He pressed his ear to the door and listened. The noises were definitely inside the attic. [*Cup ear with hand as if listening.*]

Shuffle. Shuffle. Drag. Shuffle. Shuffle. Drag . . .

Then, very quietly, he opened the door, stepped in, and . . . [*big dramatic pause*]

[*Now SCREAM LOUDLY!*] Aaaaaaaaaaaaaaaaaaaaaaaaaaaaaaah!

[*Then don't say anything else. Stop as though you have finished telling the story. Inevitably, someone will ask, "Why did he scream?" You answer:*]

You would scream too, if you stepped on a nail in your bare feet!

18

Blood Red Lips

> *Note from Dianne:* This is a fun story to draw out and tell to all ages (except the very young). It is suspenseful, and you can really play up the scary elements of the "thing" in the story. It is a "shaggy dog" tale with an ending that provides comic relief.

Alice was not a very obedient girl. She didn't always listen to the rules or play by the rules. And Alice LOVED mischief. One night, at the dinner table, Alice put roast beef, mashed potatoes, and peas in her mouth, chewed it up, and then opened her mouth so she could show everyone her "dinner art." [*Mime putting food in your mouth and chewing. Then make a face and show your tongue. The audience will respond with "ewwww" and/or laughter.*]

Alice's mother said, "Alice, if you don't start behaving yourself, one day Bony Fingers will come and get you!"

Alice said, "Whatever!" [*Say "Whatever!" with attitude and your hands on your hips.*]

That night, Alice was lying in bed thinking of what kind of mischief she could make the next day. She heard a noise at her window.

Tap, tap, tappity tap, tap, tap. [*Mime knocking.*]

Tap, tap, tappity tap, tap, tap.

From *Scared Silly: 25 Tales to Tickle and Thrill* by Dianne de Las Casas. Illustrated by Soleil Lisette. Santa Barbara, CA: Libraries Unlimited/Teacher Ideas Press. Copyright © 2010.

Alice went to the window and shrieked. [*Scream.*] There at the window was an ugly old hag with long, stringy hair, big yellow eyes, and a giant wart on her chin.

She grinned at Alice with sharp green teeth. "Hello little girl! Would you like to see what I can do with my blood red lips and my long bony fingers?" [*Give the old hag a creepy, witchy voice.*]

Alice cried, "Ewwwww! NO!" She closed her curtains and climbed back into bed, shivering with fright.

By late afternoon of the next day, Alice had forgotten all about her strange nightly visitor. She was back to her usual mischief making. Her mother sent her to bed without supper.

That night, Alice was lying in bed when she heard a noise at her window.

Tap, tap, tappity tap, tap, tap. [*Mime knocking.*]

Tap, tap, tappity tap, tap, tap.

Alice went to the window and shrieked. [*Scream.*] There at the window was [*pause*] an ugly old hag with long, stringy hair, big yellow eyes, and a giant wart on her chin.

She grinned at Alice with sharp green teeth. "Hello little girl! Would you like to see what I can do with my blood red lips and my long bony fingers?"

Alice cried, "Ewwwww! NO!" She closed her curtains and climbed back into bed, shivering with fright.

The next day, Alice only made a little mischief. Her mother put her in time-out.

That night, Alice was lying in bed when she heard a noise at her window.

Tap, tap, tappity tap, tap, tap. [*Mime knocking.*]

Tap, tap, tappity tap, tap, tap.

Alice went to the window and shrieked. [*Scream.*] There at the window was [*pause*] an ugly old hag with long, stringy hair, big yellow eyes, and a giant wart on her chin.

She grinned at Alice with sharp green teeth. "Hello little girl! Would you like to see what I can do with my blood red lips and my long bony fingers?"

Alice cried, "Ewwwww! NO!" She closed her curtains and climbed back into bed, shivering with fright.

The next day, Alice was a model child. In fact, she even offered to HELP at school and at home. Alice's mother was shocked. Alice's mother gave her extra dessert.

That night, Alice was lying in bed when she heard a noise at her window.

Tap, tap, tappity tap, tap, tap. [*Mime knocking.*]

Tap, tap, tappity tap, tap, tap.

Alice went to the window and shrieked. [*Scream.*] There at the window was [*pause*] an ugly old hag with long, stringy hair, big yellow eyes, and a giant wart on her chin.

She grinned at Alice with sharp green teeth. "Hello little girl! Would you like to see what I can do with my blood red lips and my long bony fingers?"

Alice cried, "What?!! What do you do with your blood red lip and your long bony fingers?! Tell me already!"

The ugly old hag said, "Come closer, little girl . . ."

Alice leaned forward . . . and [*big pause*] . . .

The hag slowly reached up with one hand and then drummed her bony fingers on her blood red lips saying, "Bbblllbbblllbbblllbbblllbbblllbbblllbbblllbbblll!" [*Rub your finger up and down against your lips, making this sound. Repeat and have children do it with you to relieve the tension of the story.*]

Bloody Finger

Note from Dianne: This is a great "campfire" story. I first heard a version of this story in elementary school, when I was in the Girl Scouts. It's a "shaggy dog" tale that has great potential for suspense and tons of creepy shivers. Use different voices for each character in the family. Timing is everything in the end . . .

Not that long ago, a family of five—Papa, Mama, Brother, Sister, and Baby—[*Point to each finger on one hand, starting with the thumb.*] went on a spur-of-the-moment getaway. After a long day of sightseeing, the family needed a hotel. Every hotel they checked was completely booked. They came to one last hotel, and they were [*pause*] desperate!

The hotel clerk said, "I'm sorry, but we're all booked up."

Papa said, "We've checked every hotel in town, and we're desperate! We'll take anything! Don't you have even one room available?"

The clerk popped his gum. "Um. We do have one room left, but we NEVER rent it out."

Papa said, "Look, I'll pay you double for the room. We'll take it."

The clerk looked doubtful. "Okay, but I have to warn you. It is HAUNTED. [*Raise your voice.*] Those that check in, never check out!" [*Use an ominous voice.*]

From *Scared Silly: 25 Tales to Tickle and Thrill* by Dianne de Las Casas. Illustrated by Soleil Lisette. Santa Barbara, CA: Libraries Unlimited/Teacher Ideas Press. Copyright © 2010.

Papa took the key, and the family went into the room. Because they were so tired, they decided to order pizza. Mama said, "Okay, time to wash up. I'll go first."

So Mama went into the bathroom and heard a voice cry, "BLOOOODY FIIIIINNNGER! BLOOOODY FIIIIINNNGER!" [*Say this low and softly.*] She was so scared that she jumped out the window, never to be seen again.

Papa said, "Why is Mama taking so long? I'll check on her." So Papa went into the bathroom and heard a voice cry, "BLOOOODY FIIIIINNNGER! BLOOOODY FIIIIINNNGER!" [*Say this a little louder but still softly.*] He was so petrified that he jumped out the window, never to be seen again.

Brother said, "Why are Mama and Papa taking so long? I'll check on them." So Brother went into the bathroom and heard a voice cry, "BLOOOODY FIIIIINNNGER! BLOOOODY FIIIIINNNGER!" [*Draw it out more and be a little louder.*] He was so mortified that he jumped out the window, never to be seen again.

Sister said, "Why are Mama, Papa, and Brother taking so long? I'll check on them." So Sister went into the bathroom and heard a voice cry, "BLOOOODY FIIIIINNNGER! BLOOOODY FIIIIINNNGER!" [*Draw it out more and be even louder.*] She was so terrified that she jumped out the window, never to be seen again.

Baby was really HUNGRY. Where was everyone? So Baby went into the bathroom and heard a voice cry, "BLOOOODY FIIIIINNNGER! BLOOOODY FIIIIINNNGER!" [*Say this very loud. You will be increasing the intensity each time.*]

Baby heard the loud voice again. "BLOOOODY FIIIIINNNGER! BLOOOODY FIIIIINNNGER!" [*Say this extremely loud.*]

Baby just sat there sucking his thumb. This time, the loud voice boomed, "BLOOOODY FIIIIINNNGER! BLOOOODY FIIIIINNNGER!" [*Say this super loud.*]

Then Baby yelled, "BE QUIET AND PUT ON A BAND-AID!" [*Use a funny baby voice, but be VERY loud.*]

The Coffin

Note from Dianne: This is one of my favorite stories to tell to a family audience. It has elements of drama and suspense, with a funny ending. I first heard this story at a storytelling festival in Ocean Springs, Mississippi, in 1996. The teller added so much suspense that I nearly fell out of my chair several times. I fell in love with the tale and added it to my scary story repertoire. Since then, "The Coffin" has taken on a life of its own.

Twelve-year-old Billy and his parents were going on vacation. They drove up the windy mountain road to a remote, two-story cabin in the woods.

When they arrived, they unpacked. After a while, Billy's mom said, "Oh no! A storm is coming, and we forgot batteries for our flashlight. Your dad and I are going to run to the country store. You'll be okay by yourself, won't you, Billy?"

Billy said, "Mom! I'm not a baby. I can take care of myself." [*Whine when you say this.*]

Billy's mom said, "Well, alright. But remember, while we're gone, DO NOT answer the door!" [*Shake your finger at the audience.*]

Billy promised his mom, and his parents left. Outside, just as his mom predicted, a storm was brewing. Dark clouds quickly shrouded the sky. Lightning FLASHED, thunder CRASHED, and rain POURED. [*Say this with punctuated emphasis.*]

Although Billy was not a "baby," [*Say "baby" very whiney.*] he didn't like being by himself [*pause*] in a cabin [*pause*] in the woods [*pause*] during a STORM! Just then, he heard a knock on the door.

Thump! Thump! Thump!

Billy's mother had warned him before she left, "Remember, while we're gone, DO NOT answer the door!"

What do you think Billy did? [*Allow the audience to answer.*] That's right! He opened the door!

There, standing in the doorway, was a giant, seven-foot-tall, black [*pause*] COFFIN! Billy shrieked. [*You may add a shriek for a jump effect.*] He tried to close the door, but it was too late! The coffin entered the house and began chasing Billy.

BOOM! BOOM! BOOM!

BOOM! BOOM! BOOM!

[*Make the "BOOM!" sound low and ominous.*]

Billy didn't know what to do, so he ran up the stairs. Not far behind, the coffin chased Billy.

BOOM! BOOM! BOOM!

BOOM! BOOM! BOOM!

[*Make the "BOOM!" sound low but more frantic.*]

Billy didn't know what to do, so he ran into the bathroom. Closer still, the coffin chased Billy.

BOOM! BOOM! BOOM!

BOOM! BOOM! BOOM!

[*Make the "BOOM!" sound low and pick up the pacing to create tension.*]

Billy said to himself, "Think! Think! Think!" He pulled down the shower curtain and threw it over the coffin. Nothing happened. It didn't stop the coffin.

BOOM! BOOM! BOOM!

BOOM! BOOM! BOOM!

[*Say the "BOOM!" sound even faster.*]

So Billy grabbed a towel, wet it, and twisted it up. He began whipping the coffin. [*Make whipping sounds and mime whipping a twisted towel.*] Nothing happened. It didn't stop the coffin.

BOOM! BOOM! BOOM!

BOOM! BOOM! BOOM!

[*Say the "BOOM!" sound even faster and louder.*]

Finally, Billy said, "I know what to do!"

He reached into the medicine cabinet and grabbed his ultimate SECRET WEAPON! [*Say this with big emphasis.*]

He aimed and threw a . . . [*big dramatic pause*] COUGH DROP! [*Say this loud.*]

And . . . it stopped the coughin'! [*Cough, cough, cough. You may have to repeat the last line, "It stopped the coughin'!" and cough a few more times until the audience gets it and laughs.*]

The Ghost of Mable Gable

Note from Dianne: "The Ghost of Mable Gable" is probably my most popular, most requested "scared silly" story. It is a story that I heard long ago, when I was in the Girl Scouts. There are many variants, including one that ends with "I'm the ghost of Davy Crocket. Put your money in my pocket." This version is uproariously funny, and I added a few extra lines at the end to maximize on the humor. It's a perfect scared silly story for a family, campfire, or anytime setting. You'll have a great time telling this tale!

There was once a family of five. [*Hold up one hand.*] There was Papa. [*Laugh deeply.*] There was Mama [*Laugh in a high-pitched voice.*] There was Brother. [*Flex your muscles and pose in a "strong man" stance.*] There was Sister. [*Pat your hair in a prissy manner while wiggling your hips.*] And there was Baby. [*Mime rocking a baby and suck on your thumb.*]

Now this family of five [*Hold up one hand.*] had just moved to a new town and bought a new house. Only it wasn't a new house at all. It was an old Victorian house with peeling paint, missing shutters, and cracked windows. The townsfolk warned the family, "Don't move into that house, for it is haunted by the Ghost of Mable Gable."

But the family paid them no mind. They said, "Everyone knows . . . [*pause*] there are no such thing as ghosts." [*Point your index finger and wave it from side to side, signifying "no."*] They moved in anyway.

From *Scared Silly: 25 Tales to Tickle and Thrill* by Dianne de Las Casas. Illustrated by Soleil Lisette. Santa Barbara, CA: Libraries Unlimited/Teacher Ideas Press. Copyright © 2010.

One day, Papa had to fix a window in one of the upstairs rooms. He gathered his tools and walked up the stairs [*Optional: Create a rhythm for each character walking up the stairs.*]

The only thing in the room was a table. Papa began to work. That's when he noticed a LOUD [*Yell "LOUD."*] noise behind him. He turned around and saw a ghostly white woman hovering. She said:

"I'm the ghost of Mable Gable!

"Put your money on the table!" [*Say this in a lilting, ghostly voice.*]

Papa screamed like a girl and ran down the stairs. He said, "Mama, mama! Upstairs, there is a . . . [*pause*] GHOST!"

Mama laughed [*with a high-pitched laugh*]. "Papa, you've just been working too hard. Everyone knows . . . [*pause*] there are . . . no such thing as ghosts! I'll prove it to you."

So Mama walked up the stairs. [*Optional: Create a rhythm for each character walking up the stairs.*] When she got in the room, she looked around. She said, "Papa! There is nothing . . ." [*Interrupt yourself.*] Mama turned around and saw a ghostly white woman hovering. She said:

"I'm the ghost of Mable Gable!

"Put your money on the table!" [*Say this in a louder, lilting, ghostly voice.*]

Mama screamed and ran down the stairs. She said, "Papa, Papa! You are right! Upstairs, there is a . . . [*pause*] GHOST!"

Brother laughed [*with a lower-pitched laugh*]. "You guys are being silly. Everyone knows . . . [*pause*] there are . . . no such thing as ghosts! I'll prove it to you. Besides, I'm strong. HUH! [*Flex your arms like a strong man.*] and I'm not afraid."

So Brother walked up the stairs. [*Optional: Create a rhythm for each character walking up the stairs.*] When he got in the room, he looked around. He said, "Mama, Papa! There is nothing . . ." [*Interrupt yourself.*] Brother turned around and saw a ghostly white woman hovering. She said:

"I'm the ghost of Mable Gable!

"Put your money on the table!" [*Say this in an even louder, lilting, ghostly voice.*]

Brother screamed like a girl and ran down the stairs. He said, "Mama, Papa! You are right! Upstairs, there is a . . . [*pause*] GHOST!"

Sister laughed [*Give a high-pitched giggle while putting your hair and wiggling your hips*]. "You guys are being silly. Everyone knows . . . [*pause*] there are . . . no such thing as ghosts! I'll prove it to you. Besides, I'm tough and I'm not afraid."

So Sister walked up the stairs. [*Optional: Create a rhythm for each character walking up the stairs.*] When she got in the room, she looked around. She said, "Mama, Papa, Brother! There is nothing . . ." [*Interrupt yourself.*] Sister turned around and saw a ghostly white woman hovering. She said:

"I'm the ghost of Mable Gable!

"Put your money on the table!" [*Say this in an ominous, loud, ghostly voice.*]

Sister said, "I don't have any money!" She screamed and ran down the stairs. She said, "Mama, Papa, Brother! You are right! Upstairs, there is a . . . [*pause*] GHOST!"

Baby laughed [*Suck your thumb and laugh like a baby*]. "I'll go upstairs. I'm not afraid of no ghost 'cause a baby's gotta do what a baby's gotta do!" [*Say this in a very funny, babyish voice.*]

So Baby crawled up the stairs. [*Optional: Create a rhythm for each character going up the stairs.*] When Baby got in the room, he looked around. He sucked his thumb. "Mmmmmmm," he said pulling out this thumb, "I like it." [*Say this in a very babyish voice, pronouncing "like" as "yike." Then put your thumb back in your mouth.*]

Then Baby turned around and saw a ghostly white woman hovering. She said:

"I'm the ghost of Mable Gable!

"Put your money on the table!" [*Say this in a very LOUD, ominous, ghostly voice.*]

Baby said:

"Oh yeah?!!! Well, I'm the ghost of Peter Piper!!

Put your money in my diaper."

[*Say this in a very funny, babyish voice and mime as though you are pulling the back of your "diaper" out. After the laughter dies down, say:*]

Well, the Ghost of Mable Gable flew out of the window, [*pause*] never to be seen again, because let me tell you, what was in Baby's diaper was scariest of all! [*Mime pulling out a diaper again and then hold your nose and wave one hand in front of your face to signify "stinky."*]

Going on a Ghost Hunt

> *Note from Dianne:* This is a great story for pre-K to first grade. It is an adaptation of the classic, "We're Going on a Bear Hunt." There is lots of fun audience participation, and the children LOVE being a part of the story. At the beginning, have the children create a rhythm by slapping their laps and clapping their hands (lap, clap, lap, clap).

We're going on a ghost hunt.

Audience: *We're going on a ghost hunt.*

[*Keep the "lap clap" rhythm going.*]

It's such a spooky night.

Audience: *It's such a spooky night.*

[*Keep the "lap clap" rhythm going.*]

We're not afraid!

Audience: *We're not afraid!*

[*Stop the rhythm and wave a pointed finger from side to side in front of you.*]

Uh oh!

Audience: *Uh oh!*

[*Place both hands on your face and act surprised.*]

Tall, tall grass.

Audience: *Tall, tall grass.*

[*Raise your hands over your head and wiggle your fingers to symbolize grass.*]

We can't go over it.

Audience: *We can't go over it.*

[*Arch your arms over your head as if going "over."*]

We can't go under it.

Audience: *We can't go under it.*

[*Crouch low and put your arms in front of you as if going "under."*]

I guess we'll have to go [*pause*] THROUGH IT!

Swish, swish, swish, swish!

Audience: *Swish, swish, swish, swish!*

[*Raise hands over your head and "swish" them from side to side.*]

We're going on a ghost hunt.

Audience: *We're going on a ghost hunt.*

[*Keep the "lap clap" rhythm going.*]

It's such a spooky night.

Audience: *It's such a spooky night.*

[*Keep the "lap clap" rhythm going.*]

We're not afraid!

Audience: *We're not afraid!*

[*Stop the rhythm and wave a pointed finger from side to side in front of you.*]

Uh oh!

Audience: *Uh oh!*

[*Place both hands on your face and act surprised.*]

An icky, sticky mud puddle.

Audience: *An icky, sticky mud puddle.*

[*Raise your hands over your head and wiggle your fingers to symbolize grass.*]

We can't go over it.

Audience: *We can't go over it.*

[*Arch arms over your head as if going "over."*]

We can't go under it.

Audience: *We can't go under it.*

[*Crouch low and put arms in front of you as if going "under."*]

I guess we'll have to go [*pause*] THROUGH IT!

Squish, squish, squish, squish!

Audience: *Squish, squish, squish, squish!*

[*Stomp your feet and make "squishing" motions with your hands as if going through mud.*]

We're going on a ghost hunt.

Audience: *We're going on a ghost hunt.*

[*Keep the "lap clap" rhythm going.*]

It's such a spooky night.

Audience: *It's such a spooky night.*

[*Keep the "lap clap" rhythm going.*]

We're not afraid!

Audience: *We're not afraid!*

[*Stop the rhythm and wave a pointed finger from side to side in front of you.*]

Uh oh!

Audience: *Uh oh!*

[*Place both hands on your face and act surprised.*]

A cold, deep river.

Audience: *A cold, deep river.*

[*Raise your hands over your head and wiggle your fingers to symbolize grass.*]

We can't go over it.

Audience: *We can't go over it.*

[*Arch your arms over your head as if going "over."*]

We can't go under it.

Audience: *We can't go under it.*

[*Crouch low and put your arms in front of you as if going "under."*]

I guess we'll have to go [*pause*] THROUGH IT!

Splash, splash, splash, splash!

Audience: *Splash, splash, splash, splash!*

[*Move your hands up and down as if splashing in water.*]

We're going on a ghost hunt.

Audience: *We're going on a ghost hunt.*

[*Keep the "lap clap" rhythm going.*]

It's such a spooky night.

Audience: *It's such a spooky night.*

[*Keep the "lap clap" rhythm going.*]

We're not afraid!

Audience: *We're not afraid!*

[*Stop the rhythm and wave a pointed finger from side to side in front of you.*]

Uh oh!

Audience: *Uh oh!*

[*Place both hands on your face and act surprised.*]

A deep, dark forest.

Audience: *A deep, dark forest.*

[*Raise your hands over your head and wiggle your fingers to symbolize grass.*]

We can't go over it.

Audience: *We can't go over it.*

[*Arch your arms over your head as if going "over."*]

We can't go under it.

Audience: *We can't go under it.*

[*Crouch low and put your arms in front of you as if going "under."*]

I guess we'll have to go [*pause*] THROUGH IT!

Step on those branches! Crackle, crackle, crackle, crackle!

Audience: *Crackle, crackle, crackle, crackle!*

[*Step as though stepping on crackling branches.*]

We're going on a ghost hunt.

Audience: *We're going on a ghost hunt.*

[*Keep the "lap clap" rhythm going.*]

It's such a spooky night.

Audience: *It's such a spooky night.*

[*Keep the "lap clap" rhythm going.*]

We're not afraid!

Audience: *We're not afraid!*

[*Stop the rhythm and wave a pointed finger from side to side in front of you.*]

Uh oh!

Audience: *Uh oh!*

[*Place both hands on your face and act surprised.*]

A dark, haunted house!

Audience: *A dark, haunted house!*

[*Raise your hands over your head and wiggle your fingers to symbolize grass.*]

We can't go over it.

Audience: *We can't go over it.*

[*Arch your arms over your head as if going "over."*]

We can't go under it.

Audience: *We can't go under it.*

[*Crouch low and put your arms in front of you as if going "under."*]

I guess we'll have to go . . . [*Pause; the children will answer "through it." You say:*]

NO! IN IT!

Ssshhh! Tiptoe, tiptoe, tiptoe, tiptoe. [*Say this very quietly.*]

Audience: *Tiptoe, tiptoe, tiptoe, tiptoe.*

[*Tiptoe through the audience until you come to an adult. Put your hands on the adult's head and say:*]

Uh oh! It's a ghost! Oh, no! Let's go HOME!

[*The next part must be said very rapidly, along with the accompanying motions, as if you are hurrying back home.*]

Back through the deep, dark forest!

Crackle, crackle, crackle, crackle!

Through the cold, deep river . . .

Splash, splash, splash, splash!

Through the icky, sticky mud puddle . . .

Squish, squish, squish, squish!

Through the tall, tall grass . . .

Swish, swish, swish, swish!

Open the door! Close it! BAM! Lock it!

[*Mime opening, closing, and locking the door.*]

Run up the stairs!

Run, run, run, run!

[*Mime running.*]

Jump in bed. Pull the covers over your head!

[*Mime jumping in bed and pulling the covers over your head.*]

Everyone, peek out from underneath the covers!

[*Mime peeking.*]

I don't think we should go on a ghost hunt ever again!!

[*Shake your head no and wave your pointed index finger from side to side in front of you.*]

That ghost . . . [*dramatic pause*]

SLIMED ME! EWWWW! YUCK!

[*Wipe your hands on an audience member.*]

The Golden Arm

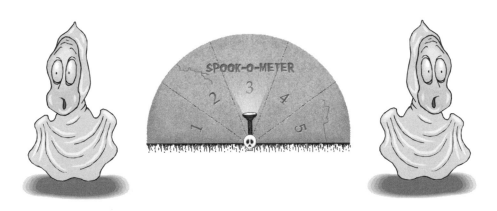

Note from Dianne: I love telling this story to an older audience. I like to draw out the elements of suspense and make Matthias as wicked as possible. Melinda, on the other hand, is a sweet wife—sweet that is, until she returns from the dead. Matthias gets what is coming to him, and so does the audience—a big JUMP.

Matthias Cranston was a wicked, wicked man. He was so wicked, in fact, that the townsfolk avoided him at all costs. When Matthias walked on one side of the street, everyone else walked on the other. More than anything, Matthias wanted a wife. But not just any wife—he wanted one who was RICH!

Melinda Joy was a sweet, sweet woman. She was so sweet, in fact, that she made everyone around her smile. When Melinda walked into a room, everyone gathered around. More than anything, Melinda wanted a husband. But not just any husband—she wanted one who didn't mind her golden arm. You see, Melinda lost her arm when she was a little girl, and her RICH father replaced it with a gleaming, golden arm.

As fate would have it, Matthias and Melinda met. They were a perfect match. Or so it seemed. Matthias wanted a woman with money, and Melinda was RICH. Melinda wanted a man who didn't mind her golden arm, and Matthias didn't mind at all. Oh no! As a matter of fact, he LOVED her gleaming, golden arm. So Matthias and Melinda got married.

From *Scared Silly: 25 Tales to Tickle and Thrill* by Dianne de Las Casas. Illustrated by Soleil Lisette. Santa Barbara, CA: Libraries Unlimited/Teacher Ideas Press. Copyright © 2010.

Every day Matthias stared at his wife. Melinda thought it was love. Oh, it was love alright, love of her gleaming, golden arm. Matthias couldn't wait until the day that gleaming, golden arm was his and ONLY his. [*Say this with greed.*]

When winter set in, suddenly and unexpectedly, Melinda died.

The entire town gathered for Melinda's funeral. There were whisperings and rumors. HOW did Melinda die? Matthias was a wicked man, and the townsfolk just KNEW it had to be his doing.

Matthias kept a vigil next to Melinda in her coffin. She was dressed in a white gown, and her gleaming, golden arm lay across her chest. Night fell, and the last mourner left the chapel. Matthias was finally alone with his dead wife. The light from the candle flickered and cast a warm glow on Melinda's golden arm. Matthias couldn't take it anymore. He reached inside the coffin and snatched the golden arm. "At last!" he cried, "It's mine, all mine!" [*Say this with greed.*]

Matthias closed the coffin and ran home. The next day, Melinda was buried. Good and buried, as far as Matthias was concerned. That night, he lay in bed with the golden arm under the pillow next to him, the pillow of his now dead wife.

Suddenly, Matthias heard a loud rattle and a ghostly howl. "Who stole my golden arm away? Who stole my golden arm away?!" [*Say this in a high, ghostly voice, drawing out the vowels.*]

Matthias said, "It's just the wind." Or so he tried to comfort himself.

There was a soft knock at the door. Again, the ghostly howl. "Who stole my golden arm away? Who stole my golden arm away?!" [*Say this in a high, ghostly voice, drawing out the vowels.*]

Then the door blew open, and a ghostly woman in a tattered white gown stood at the foot of his bed. It was his dead wife, Melinda! She howled, "Who stole my golden arm away? Who stole my golden arm away?!" [*Say this in a high, ghostly, now urgent voice, drawing out the vowels.*]

Matthias shivered. The ghost glided next to the bed and bent down. She whispered in his ear, "You'll never see the light of day. For YOU stole my golden arm away!!" [*Say this quietly until you get to "YOU," and then yell it for the jump effect.*]

From that time forward, no one ever heard from Matthias Cranston again. And no one [*pause*] ever cared. [*Punctuate the ending.*]

The Graveyard Dare

Note from Dianne: "The Graveyard Dare" is a classic urban legend. This is a great story for middle schoolers. They can relate to elements in the story because this is the age at which peer pressure comes into play, and children like to "prove" themselves by accepting bets and dares. The key to this story is the pacing. Build anxiety and urgency in the story the longer the girl is in the graveyard.

Tina and her friends walked through Old Man's Hollow on their way to a friend's house. They happened to walk by an old graveyard next to an abandoned church. The graveyard was soooooo old that it didn't even have a name.

Tyler said, "My grandpa said that if you stand on a grave after dark, the corpse inside the grave will reach up, grab you, and pull you under, never to be seen again."

Tina said, "Yeah, right!" [*Say this with attitude.*]

Abby said, "No, it's totally true. My Aunt Rita told me! It happened to her friend's daughter's best friend." Abby popped her gum and nodded her head. [*Nod your head with wide eyes and a serious look.*]

Tina stared at the graveyard. Abby whispered, "She was NEVER seen again!" [*Whisper with urgency and gravity.*]

Tyler said, "Hey, Tina. I'll give you twenty bucks if you stand on that grave right there." He pointed to a large, ominous gray tombstone. [*Point to a space in front of you.*]

From *Scared Silly: 25 Tales to Tickle and Thrill* by Dianne de Las Casas. Illustrated by Soleil Lisette. Santa Barbara, CA: Libraries Unlimited/Teacher Ideas Press. Copyright © 2010.

"In fact, I DARE you! Of course, you're probably *chicken*," taunted Tyler.

Tina crossed her arms. "You are all so silly. There are no such things as ghosts, monsters, or things that go BUMP in the night. And, by the way, I am NOT scared. I LIVE for danger!" Tina laughed. [*Utter a crazed laugh.*]

Tyler handed her a pocket knife. "Okay, we're heading to Todd's house. Stick a knife in that grave, [*Point to a space in front of you.*] and on the way back, we'll check for it. If we see my knife, we'll know you stood on the grave."

Tina didn't really want to accept the dare, but all her friends were staring at her, waiting. Tina grabbed the knife. "Fine!" she said, "I'll be laughing all the way to the bank!"

Tina watched her friends disappear down the road. She walked inside the graveyard and over to the large gray tombstone. The moon shone high in the sky, and a slight breeze rustled through the trees. [*Make soft wind sounds.*] An owl hooted. [*Hoot like an owl.*]

Tina talked to herself. She chanted over and over, "I am so not afraid. I am SO not afraid." She couldn't even convince HERSELF that she was brave. The truth was—Tina was totally TERRIFIED!

A twig snapped in half, [*Make a snapping twig sound.*] and the breeze rushed through the trees. [*Make louder wind sounds.*]

Tina chanted over and over, "I am so not afraid. I am SO not afraid."

Shadows darted in and out of the tombstones. The breeze rumbled through the trees. [*Make even louder wind sounds.*]

Tina couldn't take it anymore! She took the knife and plunged it into the grave. She turned to run . . . [*pause*] BUT she couldn't move. Some ONE or . . . [*pause*] some THING caught her. Tina screamed. [*Big loud scream!*]

Later that night, Tina's friends walked through Old Man's Hollow on their way home. They stopped at the old graveyard next to the abandoned church. There on the grave beneath the large gray tombstone was Tina sprawled across the grave. Tina was . . . [*pause*] DEAD. [*Say loudly and with emphasis.*]

Tina didn't know it, but she had inadvertently STABBED herself. Or at least her clothes. She had plunged the knife through her skirt, pinning it to the grave. It was only the knife that "grabbed" Tina. You see, Tina scared herself [*pause*] to DEATH. [*End with a maniacal laugh.*]

The Great Big Hairy Toe

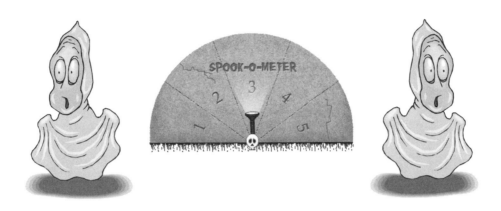

> *Note from Dianne:* "The Great Big Hairy Toe" is a loosely adapted American version of "Taily Po." It is a classic jump story. It makes a great campfire, slumber, rainy day, or any day story. Because a "great big hairy toe" is intrinsically funny, this tale is great for younger audiences. You can really ham it up until the final moments when you execute the "gotcha!" jump.

There was once a woman who found a GREAT BIG HAIRY TOE sticking out of her garden. She gave it a great big jerk and pulled it out. So the woman took the GREAT BIG HAIRY TOE home and she [*pause*] COOKED it! Then she set the table and she [*pause*] ATE it! [*Be prepared for a lot of "ewwwws" and/or laughter from your audience.*]

It sure was tasty. Yum! Yum! Yum! [*Rub your belly with each "Yum!"*] Then the woman went to bed.

Outside, the wind picked up and howled.

Hoooooooooooooooooooooooooooooooooo

Hoooooooooooooooooooooooooooooooooo

[*Invite the audience to join in the howling wind.*]

Then, in the distance, a voice cried out,

"Whose got my great big hairy toe? Whose got my great big hairy toe?!!"

[*Say this softly and draw out the long vowel "O" in each "toe."*]

From *Scared Silly: 25 Tales to Tickle and Thrill* by Dianne de Las Casas. Illustrated by Soleil Lisette. Santa Barbara, CA: Libraries Unlimited/Teacher Ideas Press. Copyright © 2010.

The woman buried herself under her blanket and said, with her fingers in her ears:

"La! La! La! La! La! La!"

"La! La! La! La! La! La!"

[*Do this part very comically. The woman is trying to drown out the sound.*]

Outside, the rain began to fall. [*Clap your hands softly against your thighs and invite the audience to join in.*] And the wind continued to howl.

Hooooooooooooooooooooooooooooooooo

Hooooooooooooooooooooooooooooooooo

Then, closer than before, a voice cried out,

"Whose got my great big hairy toe? Whose got my great big hairy toe?!!"

[*Say this louder and draw out the long vowel "O" in each "toe."*]

The woman buried herself even deeper under her blanket and said, with her fingers in her ears:

"La! La! La! La! La! La!"

"La! La! La! La! La! La!"

[*Do this part even more exaggeratedly.*]

Outside, the thunder roared. BOOM! [*Clap your hands while simultaneously yelling "BOOM!" and repeat. The audience will join in.*] The rain fell. [*Clap your hands softly against your thighs.*] And the wind continued to howl.

Hooooooooooooooooooooooooooooooooo

Hooooooooooooooooooooooooooooooooo

Then it was quiet. [*Pause for three seconds of silence, cupping your ear with a hand to listen.*] Inside the house, right next to her [*pause*] BED a voice cried out,

"Whose got my great big hairy toe? Whose got my great big hairy toe?!!"

[*Say this VERY loudly and draw out the long vowel "O" in each "toe."*]

The woman peeked out from under her blanket and a GREAT BIG HAIRY THING said, [*Say this quietly.*]

"YOU DO!" [*Yell out the last two words, causing the audience to jump.*]

The Green, Green Ribbon

> *Note from Dianne:* This is a slightly creepy story that plays on the curiosity of the listeners. You may choose to make the end dramatic, causing the audience to jump. Or you may create a quiet ending, making it more macabre.

Victoria was a BEAUTIFUL little girl. She had porcelain skin, rose red lips, and ebony black hair. She loved wearing beautiful, ruffled dresses. But there was something *different* about her. Victoria ALWAYS wore a green, green ribbon around her neck. [*Use your index finger to motion from one side of the neck to the other.*]

Edward was a CURIOUS little boy. He had chocolate brown eyes, dark dotty freckles, and curly orange hair. He loved playing on the swings and the slide at the playground. But there was something special about Edward. He LIKED Victoria. [*Emphasize "LIKED." Be prepared for a few "ewwws" from the children as well as laughter.*]

When Victoria sat on the swings, Edward sat next to her. When Victoria slid down the slide, Edward was right behind her. Soon, Victoria and Edward liked EACH OTHER. [*Emphasize "EACH OTHER." Be prepared for more "ewwws" from the children as well as laughter.*] But Edward was CURIOUS.

One day, Edward asked Victoria, "Why oh why do you wear that green, green ribbon?" [*Use your index finger to motion from one side of the neck to the other.*]

From *Scared Silly: 25 Tales to Tickle and Thrill* by Dianne de Las Casas. Illustrated by Soleil Lisette. Santa Barbara, CA: Libraries Unlimited/Teacher Ideas Press. Copyright © 2010.

Victoria batted her eyelashes and smiled sweetly. "One day, one day, you will know." [*Use a soft, creepy voice. This foreshadows the macabre ending.*]

Eventually, as boys and girls do, Edward and Victoria grew up. And they STILL liked each other. In fact, they LOVED each other. [*Emphasize "LOVED." Be prepared for even more "ewwws" from the children as well as laughter.*] So Edward and Victoria got MARRIED.

When Victoria cooked dinner, Edward washed the dishes. When Victoria washed the clothes, Edward folded the clothes. But Edward was still CURIOUS.

One day, Edward asked Victoria, "Why oh why do you wear that green, green ribbon?" [*Use your index finger to motion from one side of the neck to the other.*]

Victoria batted her eyelashes and smiled sweetly. "One day, one day, you will know." [*Use a softer, even creepier voice.*]

Eventually, as men and women do, Edward and Victoria grew old. In fact, Victoria became so sick, she lay in her death bed. [*Sputter and cough.*]

Edward stayed by her side day and night. When Victoria smiled, Edward smiled. When Victoria sighed, Edward sighed. But Edward was still CURIOUS.

One morning, Edward asked Victoria, "Why oh why do you wear that green, green ribbon?" [*Use your index finger to motion from one side of the neck to the other.*]

Victoria looked Edward in his chocolate brown eyes and said, "It is time for you to know. [*pause*] Untie the green, green ribbon."

Edward reached over and slowly, carefully, [*Draw out the words "slowly" and "carefully."*] he untied the ribbon.

Victoria's head fell . . . THUMP . . . [*The THUMP can be loud, making the audience jump, or it can be soft, making them think.*] on the floor . . . [*pause*] and rolled away. [*Say this in a quiet voice.*]

The Gunny Wolf

> *Note from Dianne:* This cautionary tale is full of action. It is not a "scary" story per se, but it does frighten small children because of the appearance of the "Gunny Wolf." Traditionally, wolves are used in stories to frighten children into submission (Think "Little Red Riding Hood" and "The Three Little Pigs.") This story can be fun or frightening, depending on how you play the Gunny Wolf. This is at the teller's discretion. The instructions in this story are for the slightly scarier version. Adjust as needed. When the little girl runs away from the Gunny Wolf, make each successive "pit-a-pat" and "hunka-cha" faster and faster.

One day, the little girl was home by herself. Her mother warned her, [*Shake your finger at the children.*] "Whatever you do, do not go outside!"

The little girl saw some beautiful white flowers by the edge of the forest. Forgetting her mother's warning, she neared the woods and picked the flowers. [*Bend down and mime picking flowers.*] Just beyond, she saw pretty pink flowers. [*Bend down and mime picking flowers.*] She picked them, too. Still deeper in the forest, she saw bright yellow flowers. [*Bend down and mime picking flowers.*] She picked them, too, singing, "Tray bla. Kee wa. Kum kwa. Kee ma."

Suddenly, the BIG BAD Gunny Wolf appeared. [*Make a snarling face and raise your arms overhead.*] He said, "Sing that guten, sweeten song again."

So the little girl began singing, "Tray bla. Kee wa. Kum kwa. Kee ma."

The Gunny Wolf fell asleep and the little girl began running away:

From *Scared Silly: 25 Tales to Tickle and Thrill* by Dianne de Las Casas. Illustrated by Soleil Lisette. Santa Barbara, CA: Libraries Unlimited/Teacher Ideas Press. Copyright © 2010.

Pit-a-pat. Pit-a-pat. Pit-a-pat. Pit-a-pat. [*Pat your hands against your thighs in a rapid motion, to the beat of "pit-a-pat."*]

The Gunny Wolf woke up and began chasing the girl.

Hunka-cha. Hunka-cha. Hunka-cha. Hunka-cha. [*Mime running to the rhythm of "hunka-cha."*]

When he caught up to the little girl, he said, "Little girl, why for you move?"

She said, "I no move."

The Gunny Wolf said, "Sing that guten, sweeten song again."

So the little girl began singing, "Tray bla. Kee wa. Kum kwa. Kee ma."

The Gunny Wolf fell asleep again, and once more, the little girl began running away:

Pit-a-pat. Pit-a-pat. Pit-a-pat. Pit-a-pat. [*Pat your hands against your thighs in a rapid motion, to the beat of "pit-a-pat."*]

The Gunny Wolf woke up and began chasing the girl.

Hunka-cha. Hunka-cha. Hunka-cha. Hunka-cha. [*Mime running to the rhythm of "hunka-cha."*]

When he caught up to the little girl, he said, "Little girl, why for you move?"

She said, "I no move."

The Gunny Wolf said, "Sing that guten, sweeten song again."

So the little girl began singing, "Tray bla. Kee wa. Kum kwa. Kee ma."

The Gunny Wolf fell asleep again, and once more, the little girl began running away:

Pit-a-pat. Pit-a-pat. Pit-a-pat. Pit-a-pat. [*Pat your hands against your thighs in a rapid motion, to the beat of "pit-a-pat."*]

The Gunny Wolf woke up and began chasing the girl.

Hunka-cha. Hunka-cha. Hunka-cha. Hunka-cha. [*Mime running to the rhythm of "hunka-cha."*]

The little girl kept running, with the Gunny Wolf chasing her.

Pit-a-pat. Pit-a-pat. Pit-a-pat. Pit-a-pat. [*Pat your hands against your thighs in a rapid motion, to the beat of "pit-a-pat."*]

Hunka-cha. Hunka-cha. Hunka-cha. Hunka-cha. [*Mime running to the rhythm of "hunka-cha."*]

Finally, she reached her house, opened the door, and slammed it tight.

BOOM! [*Raise your voice.*]

Since then, the little girl has never entered the forest and ALWAYS heeds her mother's warnings.

The Hitchhiker

Note from Dianne: "The Hitchhiker" is a classic urban legend. It is not a story filled with sound effects, audience participation, or .jumps. It is an eerie story that causes audiences to think. It buries itself in the brain, emerging when the time is right, like when you are traveling down a lonely, dark road. That being said, it is a story meant for older children—those who enjoy thrills and chills. Tell it as a "true" ghost story, using local names, landmarks, and weather. Those details add to the flavor of this story, making it accessible and even spookier.

It was late, and Steven was driving home down a long, dark stretch of road next to Bayou Black. No cars appeared for miles. Steven's thoughts were interrupted by a sudden downpour. He turned on his windshield wipers and slowed down. No, it wouldn't be cool to fishtail and end up in the bottom of the bayou.

The rain created a palpable chill in the air. He was glad he had his leather jacket on. Even in the sultry South, winters could be cold. It was a humid cold, the kind that penetrates your bones. [*Painting details like this creates realism in the story. Create the kind of road conditions that could allow a person to "see" more than he anticipated.*]

Steven drove in silence for a few miles, hearing only the syncopated drumming of rain on his car, creating a lulling rhythm. It was the kind of lullaby that creates a sense of false security. [*This foreshadows the upcoming action in the story.*]

It was then that he saw HER in the distance. Did his eyes deceive him?!! Just ahead, a girl in a long white dress [*A "white" dress is always ghostly, especially at night.*] was walking on the side of the road [*pause*] in the RAIN [*pause*] without an umbrella! [*Say this in disbelief, as if to say, "Who would walk by herself, in the cold rain without an umbrella, at this time of the night?"*]

It wasn't safe for anyone to be alone outside in this weather! So Steven slowed to a stop ahead of the young woman. He waited for her to approach the car. After a minute, she knocked on the window. [*Mime knocking. You may add a soft knocking sound effect if desired.*] He rolled down the window and stared at her. Even with her wet hair clinging to the sides of her face, she was beautiful!

Steven stammered, "Do, do you need a ride?"

The girl nodded. Steven said, "Please come in."

Instead of getting in the front seat, the girl opened the back passenger door and sat in the back seat. [*Mime the action of opening the door and getting in the car.*] Steven could see her in his rearview mirror. She was shivering. [*Mime shivering.*]

Though Steven knew the answer, he asked anyway. "Are you cold?"

The girl nodded. Steven took off his leather jacket and handed it to the girl. He tried to make small talk. "So why are you out here by yourself?"

Silence, [*big dramatic pause*] then [*pause*] . . . "I want to go home . . ." [*Say this in a dead, monotonous voice.*]

Steven said, "Sure, I'll give you a ride home. Where do you live?"

The girl pointed ahead, and all she said was, [*pause*] "I want to go home . . ." [*Say this in a dead, monotonous voice.*]

Steven was starting to get a creepy feeling in the pit of his stomach. He didn't know why. The girl had done nothing to him and yet [*pause*] . . . there was something STRANGE about her. He couldn't put his finger on it.

Steven said, "I am going to take you home, but I need to know exactly where you live. Can you tell me?"

The girl pointed ahead to a gravel road and all she said was, [*pause*] "I want to go home . . ." [*Say this in a dead, monotonous voice.*]

Steven was getting frustrated. "So do I turn here?"

Steven looked in his rearview mirror. The girl nodded. [*pause*] "I want to go home . . ." [*Say this in a dead, monotonous voice.*]

Steven gulped. He followed the gravel road, the gnawing in the pit of his stomach growing stronger. As he rounded a bend, he saw a small, white, decrepit house. He stopped in front of the house. Normally, he would open the door for the girl, but Steven couldn't get himself to move.

He looked in the rearview mirror again and the girl was . . . [*big dramatic pause*] GONE! Steven floored the gas and sped off, eager to get home.

The next day, when Steven got up, he went over the previous night's events in his head. How silly of him to be creeped out by a beautiful, harmless girl! Of course he didn't hear her leave the car. It was pouring. He started to feel better when he realized something . . . [*pause*] she had taken his leather jacket!

"Oh, no!" Steven groaned. "I've got to get my jacket back!" It was an expensive jacket, given to him as a gift when he graduated. He definitely wanted it back. So Steven returned to the gravel road and found the small, white, decrepit house.

He knocked on the door. An old lady with a sweet face answered. She seemed delighted that she had a visitor. "Hello!" she chirped.

"Hello, ma'am. My name is Steven. Last night, I gave a young girl a ride home. I was wondering if I could speak to her? I lent her my leather jacket, and she still has it."

The old woman beckoned Steven inside. "Please come in. I'll make us some tea."

Steven entered the house and followed her into an old-fashioned parlor. The old woman shuffled to the kitchen, leaving Steven alone. He glanced around the room. On a mantle over a rarely used fireplace was a picture of beautiful girl with porcelain skin and dark hair.

Steven was staring at the picture when the old woman came back with a tray loaded with a pitcher and two glasses. She said, "Oh, that's my daughter, Caroline."

Steven was puzzled. Daughter? The girl in the photo was the very same girl [*Puncuate "very same girl."*] who had been in his car last night.

The old woman picked up the picture and lovingly caressed the glass. She placed it back on the mantle. The old woman smiled at Steven. "Caroline died exactly 50 years ago in an accident on Bayou Black Road. Every year, on the anniversary of her death, she returns *home* and brings me a new visitor."

Steven refused to believe what he was hearing! "No! That can't be! I picked her up last night and brought her here. She was ALIVE." [*Place big emphasis on "ALIVE."*]

The old woman stopped smiling. [*Change your tone of voice from sweet to ominous.*] "Caroline is . . . [*pause*] DEAD. [*Place big emphasis on "DEAD."*] See for yourself! Her grave is behind our house in the family cemetery."

Steven ran out the door and followed a path behind the house. He saw the family plot. His eyes scanned the overgrown graveyard and that's when he saw it . . . . [*big dramatic pause*]

His leather jacket was folded neatly on top of a tombstone that read "Caroline Boudreaux. R.I.P." On top of the jacket was a folded piece of paper.

Steven's hands shook as he retrieved his jacket and the note. He ran to his car and sat down, panting. [*Mime opening the note.*] He slowly opened the note. . . . It said:

THANK YOU

In . . . [*big dramatic pause*] BLOOD! [*For a small startle effect, say "BLOOD!" loudly.*]

I Know an Old Lady Who Swallowed a Cat

Note from Dianne: This is my original adaptation of "I Know an Old Lady Who Swallowed a Fly." It's a fun story to tell to the very young (pre-K, kindergarten, and first grade). It's also a great warm-up for a family spooky story event.

I know an old lady who swallowed a cat. [*Say, "meow" and make a clawing motion.*]

Imagine that, to swallow a cat!

Now why, oh why, would she do that? [*Invite the audience to join in.*]

I know an old lady who swallowed a spider,

That crept and crawled and clambered inside her. [*Make crawling motions with both hands.*]

She swallowed the spider to scare the cat,

Now why, oh why, would she do that?

I know an old lady who swallowed a witch.

It caused quite an itch when she swallowed the witch. [*Scratch yourself wildly all over.*]

She swallowed the witch to hex the spider,

That crept and crawled and clambered inside her. [*Make crawling motions with both hands.*]

She swallowed the spider to scare the cat,

Now why, oh why, would she do that?

I know an old lady who swallowed a ghost.

It tickled the most when she swallowed the ghost. [*Pretend to tickle an audience member and laugh.*]

She swallowed the ghost to spook the witch,

She swallowed the witch to hex the spider,

That crept and crawled and clambered inside her. [*Make crawling motions with both hands.*]

She swallowed the spider to scare the cat,

Now why, oh why, would she do that?

I know an old lady who swallowed a vampire.

Set her stomach on fire when she ate the vampire. [*Wiggle your fingers like fire in front of your stomach.*]

She swallowed the vampire to bite the ghost.

She swallowed the ghost to spook the witch.

She swallowed the witch to hex the spider,

That crept and crawled and clambered inside her. [*Make crawling motions with both hands.*]

She swallowed the spider to scare the cat,

Now why, oh why, would she do that?

I know an old lady who swallowed a bone.

It caused her to moan when she swallowed that bone. [*Hold your stomach and moan.*]

She swallowed the bone to rattle the vampire,

She swallowed the vampire to bite the ghost,

She swallowed the ghost to spook the witch,

She swallowed the witch to hex the spider,

That crept and crawled and clambered inside her, [*Make crawling motions with both hands.*]

She swallowed the spider to scare the cat,

Now why, oh why, would she do that?

I know an old lady who swallowed a house!

Could have eaten a mouse, but she gobbled a house! [*Clap your hands repeatedly like a mouth eating and make gobbling noises.*]

She swallowed the house to settle the bone,

She swallowed the bone to rattle the vampire,

She swallowed the vampire to bite the ghost,

She swallowed the ghost to spook the witch,

She swallowed the witch to hex the spider,

That crept and crawled and clambered inside her. [*Make crawling motions with both hands.*]

She swallowed the spider to scare the cat,

Now why, oh why, would she do that?

I know an old lady who swallowed a corpse.

Now guess what? She's full of corpse!!

Rap, Rap, Rap

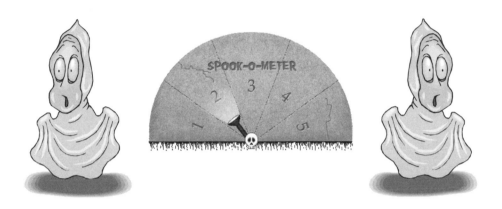

Note from Dianne: This story is great for comic relief. It's perfect to relieve the tension at the end of a long scary story session. This is also a great anytime spooky tale and works well with all ages and is a perennial favorite. I love drawing out the suspense in this story.

John worked the GRAVEYARD shift. He left work early, around 3 a.m., and drove his truck down a lonely country road through woods on either side of the road. He saw no cars for miles. He was jammin' to his favorite song [*You can be silly and dance, singing a popular radio tune.*] on the radio. Suddenly, he heard a big explosion. [*Make an explosion sound.*] Smoke rose from his hood, and his truck rolled to a stop. [*Make weird car noises, with one last explosion.*]

"Just my luck!" said John. He pulled out his cell phone and flipped it open, but it was [*pause*] DEAD.

"Oh, fiddlesticks!" yelled John. "Well, at least I have my flashlight. He reached under the seat and pulled it out. He flipped the switch on, but it was [*pause*] DEAD.

John got out of the truck. He opened the hood and a huge puff of smoke [*Puff!*] hit him in the face. There was no way he could fix his truck. He needed help. So John began walking down the road. He noticed a gravel road leading into the woods. He decided to follow it. It was his only hope. The gravel crunched under his boots.

From *Scared Silly: 25 Tales to Tickle and Thrill* by Dianne de Las Casas. Illustrated by Soleil Lisette. Santa Barbara, CA: Libraries Unlimited/Teacher Ideas Press. Copyright © 2010.

Crunch. Crunch. Crunch. [*Mime walking.*]

John continued walking until he came to a clearing and saw a white house in the distance. As he neared the house, he saw that it was in bad need of repair. The paint was peeling, the shutters hung on one hinge, and the windows were cracked. He pounded on the door.

Knock. Knock. Knock. [*Mime knocking on a door.*]

The door opened [*creaaaaaaaak*] but there was [*pause*] no one THERE! John called out, "Hello, is anyone here? I need to use the phone to call for help. My truck broke down."

No answer. So John went inside. He found matches next to a candlestick on the dining room table. He lit the candle. [*Make the sound of a match lighting. Chish!*] The flame cast shadows on the wall, and he noticed a phone. He picked it up but it was [*pause*] DEAD.

That's when John heard the sound.

Rap. Rap. Rap. [*Say this quietly.*]

Rap. Rap. Rap.

It was coming from UPSTAIRS, so John followed the sound. "Hello?" When he got to the top of the stairs, he heard it again.

Rap. Rap. Rap. [*Say this quietly.*]

Rap. Rap. Rap.

It seemed to be coming from behind [*pause*] a closed DOOR. So John opened the door. [*creaaaaaaaak*] When he entered the room, he heard it again.

This time, it seemed to be coming from ABOVE. John looked up and saw something hanging from the ceiling. It was . . . [*big dramatic pause*] a STRING to pull down the attic door. So John opened the attic door, [*creaaaaaaaak*] and out tumbled a ladder leading into the attic. He heard the sound again.

Rap. Rap. Rap. [*Say this louder.*]

Rap. Rap. Rap.

John climbed up the ladder into the attic. There, he saw a . . . [*pause*] big pine box in the shape of a [*pause*] COFFIN! He heard the sound again, coming from inside the box.

Rap. Rap. Rap. [*Say this louder.*]

Rap. Rap. Rap. [*Say this even louder.*]

John's curiosity got the best of him. He found a flathead screwdriver lying next to the pine box. He began prying the box open. The nails flew out.

Pop! Pop! Pop!

Pop! Pop! Pop!

Finally, John got it open. He slid the lid and heard the sound again. It was . . . [*big dramatic pause*]

Rap. Rap. WRAPPING PAPER! [*Say "Rap, rap" in a normal voice. Yell "WRAPPING PAPER!" for the jump effect.*]

From last Christmas. Seven rolls of it.

Raw Head and Bloody Bones

Note from Dianne: This tale is for mature listeners. The title alone can conjure dreadful images even before the story begins. It is a folktale from the American South (Southerners love a good scary story!). The ending has a similar motif to "Little Red Riding Hood," and you will recognize the cautionary aspect of this tale.

Way down South, there once lived an old conjure woman. She knew magic, oh yes she did. She could make bones in a graveyard rattle, rattle, rattle, get up and dance. Her closest companion in all of the world was a razorback hog. Because he was the companion of a conjure woman, that hog could walk on two legs and talk! He wanted for nothing, and soon he grew FAT! [*Stretch your arms out to symbolize "FAT!"*]

One day, a hunter saw that FAT hog in the woods. He aimed his gun and shot him [*pause*] dead. Then the hunter skinned the hog and left his raw head and bloody bones scattered deep in the woods under the moonlight. [*Look up and raise one hand, as if pointing to the moon.*]

Later, the conjure woman called for her hog, but he didn't come. So she began searching through the woods. Soon, she came across the hog's head and bones. Well, she knew magic, oh yes she did. She said, "Raw Head and Bloody Bones, rattle, rattle, rattle. Get up and dance!" [*Call out like a chant.*]

Raw Head and Bloody Bones got up and danced! Then he conjured himself the eyes of an owl, [*Circle your hands around your eyes.*] the claws of a bear, [*Hold your hands in front of you like scratching claws.*] the tail of a raccoon, [*Motion behind you as if drawing a tail.*] and the teeth of a panther. [*Bare your teeth.*] That night, he paid that hunter a visit.

Raw Head and Bloody Bones banged on the window. BOOM! BOOM! BOOM! [*Say this very loudly.*]

When the hunter peeked out the window, he cried out, "What do you need such big eyes for?!" [*Create a timid, frightened voice for the hunter.*]

Raw Head and Bloody Bones answered, "To see your grave." [*Create a low, creepy voice for Raw Head and Bloody Bones.*]

The hunter cried out, "What do you need such big claws for?!"

Raw Head and Bloody Bones answered, "To dig your grave."

The hunter cried out, "What do you need such a long tail for?!"

Raw Head and Bloody Bones answered, "To sweep your grave."

The hunter cried out, "What do you need such big TEETH [*Act surprised.*] for?!"

Raw Head and Bloody Bones answered, "To EAT YOU UP." [*Say loudly, with each word punctuated.*]

That hunter was never seen again. But they say that Raw Head and Bloody Bones is still around. Deep in the woods, if you hear "rattle, rattle, rattle," that is Raw Head and Bloody Bones [*slight pause*] dancing under the moonlight.

The Strange Visitor

Note from Dianne: "The Strange Visitor" is a folktale from Scotland. There are other variants around the world. It a great story for younger audiences and family audiences. Even though there are separate body parts in this tale, it is not gruesome or gross. The ending can be changed to suit the listening age and maturity of your audience. You may create a "jump" tale or make it less spooky, with a funny ending. I give you two alternatives.

There was once an old woman who lived in a house by the woods. Each night, she sat by the fire, spinning her wool.

[*Invite the audience to participate in the refrain:*]

She sat and sat, and spun and spun [*Roll your hands around and around.*]

And waited for a friend to come.

One night, the door creaked open. [*Make a creaking noise.*] In came a pair of fat feet. [*Stomp your feet.*] "How very strange!" said the woman. Still she sat by the fire, spinning her wool.

She sat and sat, and spun and spun [*Roll your hands around and around.*]

And waited for a friend to come.

Again, the door creaked open. [*Make a creaking noise.*] In came a pair of short, long legs. [*March your legs.*] The long legs stuck to the fat feet. "How very strange!" said the woman. Still she sat by the fire, spinning her wool.

She sat and sat, and spun and spun [*Roll your hands around and around.*]

And waited for a friend to come.

Again, the door creaked open. [*Make a creaking noise.*] In came a pair of huge hips. [*With your hands on your hips, wiggle your hips from side to side.*] The huge hips stuck to the long legs. The long legs stuck to the fat feet. "How very strange!" said the woman. Still she sat by the fire, spinning her wool.

She sat and sat, and spun and spun [*Roll your hands around and around.*]

And waited for a friend to come.

Again, the door creaked open. [*Make a creaking noise.*] In came a wide waist. [*With your hands on your waist, make a circle with your waist.*] The wide waist stuck to the huge hips. The huge hips stuck to the long legs. The long legs stuck to the fat feet. "How very strange!" said the woman. Still she sat by the fire, spinning her wool.

She sat and sat, and spun and spun [*Roll your hands around and around.*]

And waited for a friend to come.

Again, the door creaked open. [*Make a creaking noise.*] In came a chubby chest. [*Beat your hands on your chest.*] The chubby chest stuck to the wide waist. The wide waist stuck to the huge hips. The huge hips stuck to the long legs. The long legs stuck to the fat feet. "How very strange!" said the woman. Still she sat by the fire, spinning her wool.

She sat and sat, and spun and spun [*Roll your hands around and around.*]

And waited for a friend to come.

Again, the door creaked open. [*Make a creaking noise.*] In came a pair of enormous arms. [*Stretch your arms out and shake them.*] The enormous arms stuck to the chubby chest. The chubby chest stuck to the wide waist. The wide waist stuck to the huge hips. The huge hips stuck to the long legs. The long legs stuck to the fat feet. "How very strange!" said the woman. Still she sat by the fire, spinning her wool.

She sat and sat, and spun and spun [*Roll your hands around and around.*]

And waited for a friend to come.

Again, the door creaked open. [*Make a creaking noise.*] In came a pair of heavy hands. [*Clap your hands.*] The heavy hands stuck to the enormous arms. The enormous arms stuck to the chubby chest. The chubby chest stuck to the wide waist. The wide waist stuck to the huge hips. The huge hips stuck to the long legs. The long legs stuck to the fat feet. "How very strange!" said the woman. Still she sat by the fire, spinning her wool.

She sat and sat, and spun and spun [*Roll your hands around and around.*]

And waited for a friend to come.

Again, the door creaked open. [*Make a creaking noise.*] In came a horrible HEAD. [*Roll your head from side to side.*] The horrible head stuck to the big body. "How very strange!" said the woman.

Then the woman asked, "How did you get such big feet?"

The visitor answered, "Much stomping, much stomping!" [*Stomp. Give the visitor a deep voice.*]

The woman asked, "How did you get such long legs?"

"Much running, much running!" [*Mime running.*]

The woman asked, "How did you get such huge hips?"

"Much eating, much eating!" [*Mime eating.*]

The woman asked, "How did you get such a wide waist?"

"Much bending, much bending!" [*Bend your waist side to side.*]

The woman asked, "How did you get such a chubby chest?"

"Much breathing, much breathing!" [*Take two deep breaths.*]

The woman asked, "How did you get such enormous arms?"

"Much hanging, much hanging!" [*Raise your hands overhead.*]

The woman asked, "How did you get such heavy hands?"

"Much grabbing, much grabbing!" [*Mime grabbing.*]

The woman asked, "How did you get such a horrible head?"

"Much thinking, much thinking!" [*Point to your head.*]

Then the woman asked, "Why did you come here?"

The visitor answered, "To . . . get . . . YOU!" [*Creep up to the audience and yell "YOU!"*]

Alternative ending:

Then the woman asked, "Why did you come here?"

The visitor answered, "To . . . get . . . a . . . HUG!" [*Creep up to an audience member (a grown-up is always fun) and give that person a big hug.*]

Taily Po

> *Note from Dianne:* Taily Po is a classic jump story from the Southern United States. It is also known as "Taily Bone" and has similar elements to "The Golden Arm" and "The Hairy Toe." The setting of this story, the dark woods, gives the tale an ominous tone. The trick in telling this tale is keeping it quietly eerie until the dramatic ending. You can also tailor it for a younger audience by inviting audience participation and exaggerating the antics of the creature in the tale.

Not long ago, deep in the woods, on a cold moonlit night, a man lived all by himself. [*Begin the story quietly to set the tone. Emphasize "all by himself" so that the audience understands he is alone.*] He lived in one room, and that one room was his whole house. In it, he had a bed, a table, a chair, a sink, and a stove. On top of the stove boiled a big pot of stew. [*Emphasize the word "stew." It becomes important later in the story.*]

The man was sitting at the table, when he saw two large yellow eyes staring at him [*Circle your hands around both eyes.*] from a dark corner in the room. The creature jumped out and howled, "Yeowwwwwwww!" sounding like a tortured cat. [*Do a soft "yeow" so that you don't spoil the big jump later in the story.*]

The man was so frightened that he grabbed his axe and swung. "THUNK!" [*Mime swinging an axe.*]

He chopped off the creature's tail, and the tail landed right in the man's pot of boiling stew. The creature scampered out of the window, and the man sat back down at the table.

"Whew!" he said to no one in particular. "That was close!" Since he was hungry, he decided to eat his stew, tail and all. [*Punctuate "tail and all."*] In fact, the stew was the most delicious concoction he had ever tasted, so he slurped, slurped, slurped [*You may accompany this with slurping sounds.*] it all up.

Full and happy, the man went to bed. [*If you want to make it comical, add snoring sounds.*] He hadn't been sleeping long when he heard a strange sound on the roof.

Thump, Thumpity, Thump.

Thump, Thumpity, Thump.

[*To decrease the terror of the story, you can invite the audience to participate.*]

Then he heard a voice rustle like the breeze:

"Taily po! Taily po! Give me back my taily po!"

[*Say this softly and draw out the long vowel "A" in each "taily" and the long vowel "O" in each "po."*]

The man was a little nervous, so he snuggled deep under his covers and closed his eyes, hoping the noise would disappear. It wasn't long before he heard a strange sound on the door.

Scratch, Scratchity, Scratch.

Scratch, Scratchity, Scratch.

Then he heard a voice howl like the wind:

"Taily po! Taily po! Give me back my taily po!"

[*Say this a little louder and draw out the long vowel "A" in each "taily" and the long vowel "O" in each "po."*]

The man was really scared now. He snuggled even deeper under his covers and closed his eyes, hoping the wretched noise would disappear. It wasn't long before he heard a strange sound inside his . . . HOUSE!

Stomp, Stompity, Stomp.

Stomp, Stompity, Stomp.

The man peeked out from under his covers and saw two large yellow eyes staring at him from the foot of the bed. Then he heard a voice boom like thunder:

"Taily po! Taily po! Give me back my taily po!"

[*Say this very loudly and draw out the long vowel "A" in each "taily" and the long vowel "O" in each "po."*]

The man said quietly, his voice stuttering, "I-I-I-I don't have it!"

The creature crept across the bed and, with his large yellow eyes, looked the man dead in his eyes. He said, "Yes, you DO!" [*Yell "DO!" for the jump effect.*]

Then he grabbed the man, turned him upside down, and shook, shook, shook [*Punctuate each "shook" and mime shaking.*] him until that tail fell out in one [*pause*] whole [*pause*] piece.

The creature grabbed his taily po and scampered out of the window. The man never saw the creature again and vowed never ever EVER [*Emphasize last "EVER."*] to eat another bite of [*pause*] stew [*Emphasize "stew."*] again. Sometimes, deep in the woods, on a cold moonlit night, you can hear a voice rustle like the breeze:

"Taily po! Taily po! Now I've got my taily po!"

[*You may end this in one of two ways. (1) Choose a quiet, ghostly ending, drawing out the "O" in "po." (2) Add a second jump by yelling out "PO!" at the very end.*]

The Teeny-Tiny Woman

> *Note from Dianne:* "The Teeny-Tiny Woman" is an old English folktale. It is perfect for very young audiences such as pre-K, kindergarten, and first grade. The repetition of "teeny-tiny" makes it funny and comforting. There is a jump at the end of the story that is quite unexpected. You may tailor the "size" of the jump to the "size" of your voice. Here's a teeny-tiny bit of advice: Have fun!

Once upon a time, there was a teeny-tiny woman. [*Say "teeny-tiny" in a small voice each time.*] This teeny-tiny woman lived in a teeny-tiny house. This teeny-tiny house was in a teeny-tiny village.

One day this teeny-tiny woman put on her teeny-tiny bonnet. She left her teeny-tiny house to take a teeny-tiny walk. She walked a teeny-tiny woman when she came to a teeny-tiny gate. So the teeny-tiny woman opened the teeny-tiny gate, and entered a teeny-tiny churchyard. In that teeny-tiny churchyard, she saw a teeny-tiny bone. That teeny-tiny bone was on a teeny-tiny grave. Well the teeny-tiny woman said to her teeny-tiny self, "This teeny-tiny bone will make a tasty teeny-tiny soup for my teeny-tiny supper."

So the teeny-tiny woman put the teeny-tiny bone in her teeny-tiny pocket. Then the teeny and went home to her teeny-tiny house. When the teeny-tiny woman got home to her teeny-tiny house, she was a teeny-tiny tired. She put the teeny-tiny bone into a teeny-tiny cupboard. Then she went up her teeny-tiny stairs to her teeny-tiny bed to take a teeny-tiny nap.

From *Scared Silly: 25 Tales to Tickle and Thrill* by Dianne de Las Casas. Illustrated by Soleil Lisette. Santa Barbara, CA: Libraries Unlimited/Teacher Ideas Press. Copyright © 2010.

The teeny-tiny woman had only been asleep for a teeny-tiny time, she was awakened by a teeny-tiny voice coming from the teeny-tiny cupboard. The teeny-tiny voice said:

"Give me my bone!" [*Say this in a soft but bold voice.*]

The teeny-tiny woman was a teeny-tiny bit scared, so she hid her teeny-tiny head under her teeny-tiny blanket and went back to her teeny-tiny nap. The teeny-tiny woman had only been asleep again a teeny-tiny time when the teeny-tiny voice again cried out from the teeny-tiny cupboard a teeny-tiny louder.

"Give me my bone!" [*Say this in a louder voice.*]

This made the teeny-tiny woman a teeny-tiny bit more scared, so she hid her teeny-tiny head under her teeny-tiny blanket and went back to her teeny-tiny nap. The teeny-tiny woman had only been asleep again a teeny-tiny time, the teeny-tiny voice from the teeny-tiny cupboard said again a teeny-tiny louder:

"GIVE ME MY BONE!" [*Say this in an even louder voice.*]

The teeny-tiny woman was a teeny-tiny bit more scared, but she pulled her teeny-tiny head out from under the teeny-tiny blanket, and said in her loudest teeny-tiny voice,

"TAKE IT!" [*Yell "Take it!" to create the jump effect.*]

Tilly and the Heebie-Jeebie Man

Note from Dianne: This story has many versions. I named the "bogeyman" in this story the "Heebie-Jeebie Man" because when you get scared, you get the "heebie-jeebies." The name "Heebie-Jeebie Man" is also less frightening for younger children. I added rhythm with a participatory, repetitive chant that kids love. This is a classic jump tale with tons of suspense.

Tilly was 6 years old. Her brother, Herman, was 11 years old. Do you know what 11-year-old brothers like to do to their 6-year-old sisters? [*Pause to allow the audience to chime in answers.*] They like to TEASE them. So Herman often made fun of Tilly.

"Tilly is silly! Tilly is silly!" [*Use a mocking voice and wave your fingers on each side of your head.*]

Tilly would cry, "No, I'm nooooooooooooot!" [*Make Tilly's voice very babyish.*]

School was out, and it was summertime. Herman was going away to summer camp. Tilly had a nice, long summer without her pesky brother. But, unfortunately, summer came to an end, and Herman came home.

Herman said to Tilly, "Hey, Tilly! You wanna hear a story about camp?"

Tilly loved stories, so she nodded her head up and down [*Nod your head up and down.*] and said, "Uh huh!"

From *Scared Silly: 25 Tales to Tickle and Thrill* by Dianne de Las Casas. Illustrated by Solcil Lisette. Santa Barbara, CA: Libraries Unlimited/Teacher Ideas Press. Copyright © 2010.

Well, do you know what 11-year-old brothers like to do to their 6-year-old sisters? [*Pause to allow the audience to chime in answers.*] They like to SCARE them. So Herman told Tilly about the Heebie-Jeebie Man, who had been haunting his summer camp forever. Herman said, "Every year, the Heebie-Jeebie Man picks ONE camper to follow HOME." [*Emphasize "ONE" and "HOME" to foreshadow the upcoming events.*]

Tilly was frightened. She asked, "Well, who did the Heebie-Jeebie Man follow home this year, Herman?"

Herman didn't answer. Instead, he laughed [*Laugh ominously.*] and ran off.

That night, Tilly lay upstairs in her bed, tossing and turning. She couldn't sleep. All she kept thinking about was the Heebie-Jeebie Man. Did he follow Herman home? Was he in the house? Was he coming to get HER?! [*Emphasize "HER?!"*] Tilly shivered beneath her sheets. [*Mime shivering.*]

That's when she heard the noise. A shuffling, a creeping, a creeeeeaking! [*Creak your voice when saying "creeeeeaking!"*] A voice said:

"Boom Chicka Rocka Chicka Rocka Chicka Boom!

Hey, Tilly, [*Draw out the "eee" sound in "Tilly."*] I'm coming to your room.

I said A Boom Chicka Rocka Chicka Rocka Chicka Boom!"

Tilly was NERVOUS. She pulled her blanket up to her waist and closed her eyes, wishing it would go away. "It's the Heebie-Jeebie Man," she whispered. "Please go away!"

Again, Tilly heard the noise. A shuffling, a creeping, a creeeeeaking! [*Creak your voice when saying "creeeeeaking!"*] A voice said:

"Boom Chicka Rocka Chicka Rocka Chicka Boom!

I'm on the first step and I'm coming to your room.

I said A Boom Chicka Rocka Chicka Rocka Chicka Boom!"

Tilly was ALARMED. She pulled her blanket up to her chest and called for the strongest person in her house—her [*pause*] DAD. Tilly screamed, "Daaaaaaaaaaddddddy!" [*Rock your head from side to side when yelling "Daaaaaaaaaaddddddy!"*] But her Daddy was sleeping on the other side of the house and never came.

Again, Tilly heard the noise. A shuffling, a creeping, a creeeeeaking! [*Creak your voice when saying "creeeeeaking!"*] A voice said:

"Boom Chicka Rocka Chicka Rocka Chicka Boom!

I'm on the second step and I'm coming to your room.

I said A Boom Chicka Rocka Chicka Rocka Chicka Boom!"

Tilly was SCARED. She pulled her blanket up to her chin and called for the sweetest person in her house—her [*pause*] MOM. Tilly screamed, "Mooooooommmmmy!" [*Rock your head from side to side when yelling "Mooooooommmmmy!"*] But her Mommy was sleeping on the other side of the house and never came.

Again, Tilly heard the noise. A shuffling, a creeping, a creeeeeaking! [*Creak your voice when saying "creeeeeaking!"*] A voice said:

"Boom Chicka Rocka Chicka Rocka Chicka Boom!

I'm on the third step and I'm coming to your room.

I said A Boom Chicka Rocka Chicka Rocka Chicka Boom!"

Tilly was FRIGHTENED. She pulled her blanket up to her eyes and called for the only other person in her house—her [*pause*] BROTHER. Tilly screamed, "Heeeeerrrrrmmmman!" [*Rock your head from side to side when yelling "Heeeeerrrrrmmmman!"*] But you know what 11-year-old brothers like to do to their 6-year-old sisters? [*pause*] IGNORE them! So Herman never came.

Again, Tilly heard the noise. A shuffling, a creeping, a creeeeeaking! [*Creak your voice when saying "creeeeeaking!"*] A voice said:

"Boom Chicka Rocka Chicka Rocka Chicka Boom!

Hey, Tilly, [*Draw out the "eee" sound in "Tilly."*] I'm IN your room."

[*Emphasize "IN."*]

"I said A Boom Chicka Rocka Chicka Rocka Chicka Boom!"

Tilly was terrified. She pulled her blanket over her head and closed her eyes, wishing it would go away. "It's the Heebie-Jeebie Man," she whispered. "Please go away!"

But Tilly got CURIOUS. She pulled her blanket down and peeked. Suddenly . . .

"Boom Chicka Rocka Chicka Rocka Chicka Boom! [*Say this very quietly and creepily.*]

Hey, Tilly, [*Draw out the "eee" sound in "Tilly."*]

I've got YOU!" [*Keep it quiet, and then yell YOU!, causing your audience to jump.*]

The next morning, everyone was at the table except Tilly. What happened to her? Then suddenly, Tilly came running down the stairs, panting and wide-eyed.

Her brother Herman looked and her and said,

"Hey, Tilly, Did you sleep well?

I said A Boom Chicka Rocka Chicka Rocka Chicka BOOM!"

The Viper

Note from Dianne: The trick in telling this story effectively is to draw out the suspense with vocal variation and dramatization. Two distinct voices should be used: one for the old woman and one for the viper. This story keeps audiences on the edge of their seats until the end, where there is hilarious comic relief.

There was once an old lady who lived in an apartment complex on the third floor. Every day, she sat in her rocking chair with her quilt across her lap, reading a book. She would rock back and forth, back and forth, back and forth . . . [*Move back and forth while telling this part, placing your hands together to symbolize reading a book. Have the audience move and chant "back and forth" with you.*]

"RRRRIIINNGGG!" [*Make the ring loud and startling. The audience will jump.*]

The phone rang, and the old woman answered, "Heeeeellllllll-ooooo?!" [*Use a very old lady voice and draw out the "hello." Motion picking up a phone and holding it to your ear.*]

A voice on the other end said, "The viper is coming. The viper is coming. I'm on the first floor." [*Keep your voice husky and spooky.*]

The old woman asked, "Who is the viper, and why are you coming?"

Click. The caller hung up.

Now the old woman was nervous. She put down her book. She pulled her quilt up to her waist and rocked back and forth, back and forth, back and forth . . . .

"RRRRIIINNGGG!"

The phone rang, and the old woman answered, "Heeeeellllllll-ooooo?!"

A voice on the other end said, "The viper is coming. The viper is coming. I'm on the second floor." [*Keep your voice husky and spooky, but raise it just a bit.*]

The old woman asked, "Who is the viper, and why are you coming?"

Click. The caller hung up again!

Now the old woman was REALLY nervous. She pulled her quilt up to her chin and rocked back and forth, back and forth, back and forth . . . [*Quicken the rocking motion and words to signify nervousness.*]

"RRRRIIINNGGG!"

The phone rang, and the old woman answered, "Heeeeellllllll-ooooo?!"

A voice on the other end said, "The viper is coming. The viper is coming. I'm on the third floor." [*Raise the volume of your voice for urgency.*]

But before the old woman could ask, "Who is the viper and why are you coming?" Click. The phone went [*Place a pregnant pause here.*] DEAD!

Now the old woman was downright terrified. She curled her toes, pulled her quilt up over her head, and rocked back and forth, back and forth, back and forth . . .

Suddenly, there was [pause] a knock at the door! [*Lower your voice slightly when saying, "a knock at the door!"*]

BOOM! BOOM! BOOM! [*Knock three times firmly on a hard surface or tap on the microphone. This will cause the audience to jump.*]

Do you think the old woman should get up and answer the door? [*The audience always says "No!" Wait for them to respond and then say . . .*] You're right. She shouldn't answer the door, but in these stories, they never listen to you! The old woman got up, grabbed her cane, and walked to the door. [*Walk like an old woman with a cane. Exaggerate the movement, and your audience will laugh. I usually respond in my old lady voice. "What are you laughing at? I'm old. It takes me awhile."*]

The old woman unlocked the door. [*Motion unlocking several locks while making unlocking sound effects. Then look at the audience and say with a grin . . .*] She believed in safety!

She opened the door. CREEEAAAAK! [*Make a creaky door sound effect and draw out the suspense.*]

There, standing in front of her was [*pause*] THE VIPER! [*Look at the audience with a shocked face.*]

He was a short man, about this tall. [*Put a hand to your chest to show how tall the viper is.*] He had a sponge in one hand and a bucket in the other. He said, "Hello. I am the vindow viper. I've come to vipe your vindows."

Wait Till Bubba Comes

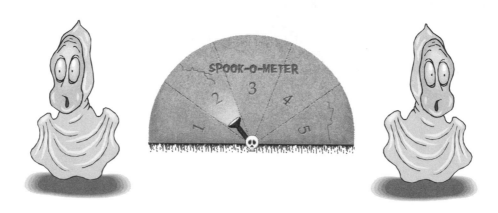

Note from Dianne: There are many versions of this story. It is most commonly known as "Wait Till Martin Comes." I think "Bubba" sounds a little more threatening, so I changed the name in this adaptation.

The large Victorian house at the end of Piney Road was haunted, and everyone knew it. Those who went inside, never came back outside.

Joe didn't believe in all that nonsense. When the townsfolk told him about the Piney Road House, Joe said, "There is no such thing as a haunted house, and I'll prove it."

He told everyone that he was going to spend the NIGHT! Joe wasn't afraid! Joe said,

"I am BIG [*Flex your arms up overhead like a strong man.*]

I am STRONG [*Flex your arms down like a strong man.*]

I'm not afraid of

Whatever comes along!"

So Joe traveled to the house on Piney Road and went inside. He built a roaring fire in the fireplace [*Wiggle your fingers in front of you and make crackling fire sounds.*] and sat down, reading a book.

Shortly after that a small black cat with green eyes sat down. He licked his paws and said,

From *Scared Silly: 25 Tales to Tickle and Thrill* by Dianne de Las Casas. Illustrated by Soleil Lisette. Santa Barbara, CA: Libraries Unlimited/Teacher Ideas Press. Copyright © 2010.

"Just you wait till Bubba comes. Just you wait till Bubba comes!" [*Say this in a creepy, quiet voice.*]

But Joe wasn't afraid! Joe said,

"I am BIG [*Flex your arms up overhead like a strong man.*]

I am STRONG [*Flex your arms down like a strong man.*]

I'm not afraid of

Whatever comes along!"

A little while later, a large black cat with yellow eyes sat down. He was the size of a big dog. He showed his claws and said,

"Just you wait till Bubba comes. Just you wait till Bubba comes!"

But Joe wasn't afraid! Joe said,

"I am BIG [*Flex your arms up overhead like a strong man.*]

I am STRONG [*Flex your arms down like a strong man.*]

I'm not afraid of

Whatever comes along!"

Not much later, a HUGE black cat with red eyes sat down. He was the size of a BULL. He opened his jaws and said,

"Just you wait till Bubba comes. Just you wait till Bubba comes!" [*Say this in a loud and ominous voice.*]

But Joe wasn't afraid! [*big dramatic pause*] Or was he? Suddenly, Joe said,

"I might be BIG [*Flex your arms up overhead like a strong man and say this in a timid voice.*]

I might be STRONG [*Flex your arms down like a strong man and say this in a timid voice.*]

But I'm not staying for

Whatever comes along!"

With that, Joe ran outside and never, ever, EVER went inside the haunted house on Piney Road again.

Who Took My Money?

> *Note from Dianne:* This is a great jump tale, very similar in style to "The Golden Arm," "Taily Po," and "The Great Big Hairy Toe." Draw out the suspense in the story and make the ending dramatic by jumping out at someone in the audience. This is a tale for older children.

An old woman got sick and died. Now, she had no children or relatives so, the neighbors took care of her. As was the custom, they dressed the old woman in her best clothes, placed her in a coffin, and set her in the living room. Well, the old woman died with her eyes wide open, as if she was staring at nothing but seeing right into your soul.

The neighbors placed two shiny gold coins on her eyelids to keep them closed. [*Make circles around your eyes with your hands.*] They lit candles and stayed with her through the night so that she wouldn't be lonely on her first night being DEAD.

Finally, it was time for the woman to be buried, so the neighbors called the gravedigger. He was about to close the casket when he noticed the two shiny gold coins on top of her eyes. [*Make circles around your eyes with your hands.*]

The gravedigger said, "Nobody will know the difference!" Then he snatched the shiny gold coins from her eyes. The woman's eyes POPPED open. Even though she was DEAD, the gravedigger had the heebie-jeebies. With her eyes wide open, it was as if she was staring at nothing but seeing right into his soul. He quickly closed the casket and took her to the cemetery.

He buried the old woman, and when he piled the last bit of dirt on her grave he said, "There. Now you're good and buried and you can't see nothin'!" [*Say this with loud emphasis.*]

When the gravedigger got home, he put those two shiny gold coins in a clear mason jar. [*Mime unscrewing a jar and placing two coins in it. Say "Clinkity clink. Clinkity clink."*] He went to bed, but he couldn't stop thinking about the DEAD old woman with her eyes wide open, as if she was staring at nothing but seeing right into his soul.

A storm started brewin' outside. The rain fell and the wind howled.

Hoooooooooooooooooooooooooo. Hoooooooooooooooooooooooooo.

[*Make the sound of the wind ghostly.*]

The coins in the mason jar began rattling.

Clinkity clink. Clinkity clink.

A voice, ever so faint, cried:

"Where are my coins, as golden as honey?

Who is the culprit that took my money?"

[*Say this in a very eerie, ghostly voice.*]

The gravedigger gulped. It couldn't be! Dead people don't just get up and [*pause*] TALK!

The storm raged outside. The rain fell and the wind howled.

Hoooooooooooooooooooooooooo. Hoooooooooooooooooooooooooo.

[*Make the sound of the wind ghostly.*]

The coins in the mason jar rattled again.

Clinkity clink. Clinkity clink.

A voice, closer now, cried:

"Where are my coins, as golden as honey?

Who is the culprit that took my money?"

[*Say this in a very eerie, ghostly voice.*]

The gravedigger was scared out of his mind. Surely, it must be his imagination! DEAD people don't just get up and [*pause*] WALK!

The storm raged outside. The rain fell and the wind howled.

Hoooooooooooooooooooooooooooo. Hoooooooooooooooooooooooooooo.

[*Make the sound of the wind ghostly.*]

The coins in the mason jar rattled yet again.

Clinkity clink. Clinkity clink.

A voice, at his door, cried:

"Where are my coins, as golden as honey?

Who is the culprit that took my money?"

[*Say this in a very eerie, ghostly voice.*]

The gravedigger was beyond terrified. He wanted to run. He wanted to hide. DEAD people don't just get up and [*pause*] KNOCK!

BOOM! BOOM! BOOM!

Then . . . [*big dramatic pause*] DEAD silence. [*Emphasize the word "DEAD."*]

A voice, inside the house, cried: [*Say this in a hushed tone.*]

"Where are my coins, as golden as honey?

Who is the culprit that took my money?"

[*Say this in a very low, creepy, ghostly voice.*]

[*Walk around as if you are blindly groping. Then yell at an audience member:*]

YOU ARE!

[*After the screams die down . . .*]

The gravedigger died with his eyes wide open, as if he was staring at nothing but seeing right into . . . [*pause*] YOUR SOUL! [*Point to an audience member.*]

Who Will Keep Me Company?

Note from Dianne: This ghostly tale preys on the psychology of being alone. I do not remember where I heard this story, but it's one of those that "stuck." It's a good creepy jump tale.

In a place called "Devil's Bluff," there lived an old woman. Her house was in the middle of the woods, and she seldom had company. Often she would make an extra bit of stew or soup, just in case someone decided to knock on her door. She was old, and she was lonely.

One night, the old woman fixed a big pot of soup. She said, "I feel it in my bones. Tonight's the night. I am going to have a visitor!"

So the old woman began rocking back and forth in her chair, knitting and singing.

"This old woman longs for a visitor in sight,

Now who will keep me company on this cold, lonely night?"

In the distance, the old woman heard a loud noise in the woods. It sounded like:

BOOM! Ka thump! BOOM! Ka thump!

BOOM! Ka thump! BOOM! Ka thump!

[*Really emphasize the spookiness of these loud sounds with your voice.*]

From *Scared Silly: 25 Tales to Tickle and Thrill* by Dianne de Las Casas. Illustrated by Soleil Lisette. Santa Barbara, CA: Libraries Unlimited/Teacher Ideas Press. Copyright © 2010.

The old woman continued rocking back and forth in her chair, knitting and singing.

"This old woman longs for a visitor in sight,

Now who will keep me company on this cold, lonely night?"

Closer now, the old woman heard a loud noise in the woods. It sounded like:

SCRATCH! Hisssssssssssssssssssssss. SCRATCH! Hisssssssssssssssssssssss.

SCRATCH! Hisssssssssssssssssssssss. SCRATCH! Hisssssssssssssssssssssss.

[*Really emphasize the spookiness of these loud sounds with your voice.*]

The old woman continued rocking back and forth in her chair, knitting and singing.

"This old woman longs for a visitor in sight,

Now who will keep me company on this cold, lonely night?"

Closer now, the old woman heard a loud in her . . . [*pause*] YARD! It sounded like:

CREAK! Rattle, rattle. CREAK! Rattle, rattle.

CREAK! Rattle, rattle. CREAK! Rattle, rattle.

[*Really emphasize the spookiness of these loud sounds with your voice.*]

The old woman continued rocking back and forth in her chair, knitting and singing.

"This old woman longs for a visitor in sight,

Now who will keep me company on this cold, lonely night?"

Suddenly, the old woman felt a hot breath on her neck. A voice said:

"I WILL!" [*Yell "I WILL!" to create the jump effect.*]

Wiley and the Hairy Man

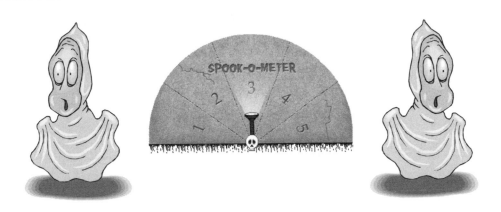

Note from Dianne: This story takes place in the swamps of the Southern United States. I like the "Southern" flair that it has. It is a lengthy story but has a lot of repetition, so it is not difficult to learn. I have added audience participation to the story. Create distinct voices for the grandmammy, Wiley, and the Hairy Man.

When Wiley's grandpappy disappeared, everyone said that the Hairy Man got him. [*Wave both arms over your head, making a scary face.*] Wiley's grandmammy would warn him, "The Hairy Man got your grandpappy and if you don't watch out, he'll get you too! Beware and take your hound dogs because the Hairy Man is scared of hound dogs." Wiley's grandmammy was from the swamps. She was real smart, and she even knew magic.

"Yes, ma'am," Wiley answered. So whenever Wiley went out, he took his hound dogs. One day, Wiley took his axe and his hound dogs to the swamp to cut some poles for a hen roost. When they got there, the hounds spotted a young pig and went chasing off after it. As Wiley was cutting down some poles, he said to himself, "I hope that Hairy Man doesn't come now, 'cause I don't have my hound dogs with me."

Sure enough, Wiley heard a strange sound. "Booga, wooga, wooga, shim bim bam, I am the Hairy Man, yes I am!" [*Invite the children to join in this participatory chorus. Say, "Please join me" and repeat the chorus.*]

From *Scared Silly: 25 Tales to Tickle and Thrill* by Dianne de Las Casas. Illustrated by Soleil Lisette. Santa Barbara, CA: Libraries Unlimited/Teacher Ideas Press. Copyright © 2010.

The Hairy Man appeared in front of Wiley. The Hairy Man was brown and HAIRY all over. [*Run a hand down each arm to indicate HAIRY.*] He had big red eyes [*With your hands, circle your eyes.*] and big yellow teeth. [*Bare your teeth.*] Worst of all, he dripped and drooled, and spit when he spoke. [*This has a rhythmic pattern.*] He was carrying a big, burlap sack. [*Hold one arm out to the side, creating a circle. Point to it with the other hand.*]

"Ooh, Hairy Man! You sure are UGLY! My grandmammy told me to stay away from you!" [*Shake your index finger three times during "stay away from you!"*]

The Hairy Man looked at Wiley and grinned with his big yellow teeth showing. [*Bare your teeth.*] He dripped and drooled, and spit when he spoke. "Wiley, I got your grandpappy, and now I'm going to get you! Just like that, jump into my sack!" [*Hold one arm out to the side, creating a circle. Point to it with the other hand.*]

Wiley looked at the Hairy Man and his sack. Then he stuck his tongue way out, like this, blew a big raspberry, [*Blow a big raspberry and ask the children to join in.*] and climbed up a cypress tree as fast as he could. [*Make climbing motions.*]

The Hairy Man said, "Booga, wooga, wooga, shim bim bam, I am the Hairy Man, yes I am! [*Repeat if necessary so the children can join in.*] Wiley, I got your grandpappy, and now I'm going to get YOU!"

The Hairy Man picked up Wiley's axe and began chop, chop, chopping away [*Make a chopping motion with one hand.*] at the cypress tree. The Hairy Man was quick, and Wiley was running out of time. The axe was nearly all the way through the tree! Poor Wiley!

Just then, Wiley could hear his hound dogs in the distance. He yelled real loud, "Heeeeeyaaaa dogs!" Quicker than the Hairy Man could blink his big red eyes, [*With your hands, circle your eyes.*] those hound dogs came running. The Hairy Man ran away.

As soon as the Hairy Man left, Wiley climbed down the tree and hastened his way to his grandmammy's house, with his hounds trailing close behind him. Wiley told his grandmammy about his narrow escape from the Hairy Man.

Grandmammy said, "Wiley, tomorrow you are going to tie up your hound dogs and face the Hairy Man. Just do as I say, do you hear me?"

Wiley exclaimed, "I'm not facing the Hairy Man by myself! He told me that he got my grandpappy, and now he's going to get me!"

But Wiley's grandmammy was from the swamps. She was real smart, and she knew magic. She said to Wiley, "When you meet up with the Hairy Man tomorrow, all you have to do is tell him he doesn't know magic. Then he'll say that he does. Bet him that he can't change into a giraffe, and then into an alligator, and then into a possum. The Hairy Man likes to show off his magic, and he'll change into all of those things. When he changes into the possum, grab his burlap sack and stuff him into it and throw him into the swamp water."

The next day, Wiley went into the swamps. Sure enough, he heard that strange sound, "Booga, wooga, wooga, shim bim bam, I am the Hairy Man, yes I am!" [*Pause after "strange sound" so that the children will have a chance to join in the refrain.*]

Wiley stood face to face with the Hairy Man, staring at his big red eyes [*With your hands, circle your eyes.*] and looking at his large yellow teeth. [*Bare your teeth.*] Wiley said, "I bet you don't know magic."

The Hairy Man looked at Wiley and said, [*pause*] "Booga, wooga, wooga, shim bim bam, I am the Hairy Man, yes I am! And the Hairy Man knows plenty of magic!"

"Then show me!" said Wiley. "I bet you can't change into a tall giraffe!

Quicker than Wiley could blink his eyes, the Hairy Man changed into a tall giraffe, taller than the cypress trees in the swamp. [*Raise your hands high in the air to signify "tall."*] Wiley said, "Well, I bet you can't change into an alligator!"

Quicker than Wiley could blink his eyes, the Hairy Man changed into a big alligator with sharp teeth. [*Make a chomping gator by clapping your hands together in a large motion, straight in front of you.*] Then Wiley said, "Well, I bet you can't change into a possum!" [*Put one arm behind you and swish from side to side like a possum's tail.*]

Quicker than Wiley could blink his eyes, the Hairy Man changed into a small possum with a hairless tail. Wiley grabbed the Hairy Man's burlap sack and said, "Just like that, jump into this sack!" [*Hold one arm out to the side, creating a circle. Point to it with the other hand.*] He threw the Hairy Man possum inside the sack, tied it up, and threw the sack into the swamp water. [*Mime throwing a sack into the water.*]

But the Hairy Man knew magic. He changed himself into the wind and blew right out of the sack. He stood in front of Wiley and said, [*pause*] "Booga, wooga, wooga, shim bim bam, I am the Hairy Man, yes I am! Wiley, I got your grandpappy, and now I'm going to get you!"

The Hairy Man picked Wiley up and threw him into the burlap sack, tied it up with rope, and said, "Just like that, jump into my sack." [*Hold one arm out to the side, creating a circle. Point to it with the other hand.*]

But Wiley was smart like his grandmammy. "Hairy Man," Wiley yelled through the bag, "I bet you can't make all the rope in the parish disappear."

Hairy Man stopped and set the bag down. "Oh, yeah? I can do any kind of magic! Now all of the rope in the parish has disappeared."

Wiley climbed out of the burlap sack and yelled, "Heeeeeyaaaa dogs!" And quicker than the Hairy Man could blink his big red eyes [*With your hands, circle your eyes.*], those hound dogs, who weren't tied up any more because of the Hairy Man's magic, came running. The Hairy Man ran away.

Wiley hurried home with his hound dogs trailing behind him. When he got home, Wilee told the whole story to his grandmammy.

Grandmammy said, "Well, Wiley, you fooled that Hairy Man two times. Fool him one more time, and he'll never bother you again. The Hairy Man's going to come back tomorrow, but I am from the swamps. I'm smart, and I know magic. I have a plan."

Sure enough, the next day Wiley and his grandmammy heard a strange noise at the door. [*Pause so the children can join in.*] "Booga, wooga, wooga, shim bim bam, I am the Hairy Man, yes I am! Wiley, I got your grandpappy and now I'm going to get you!" [*This will be the last time the Hairy Man says this, so you can intensify your voice and make it more gruff and scary to heighten the drama.*]

Grandmammy yelled at the Hairy Man through the door. "If I give you my baby, will you leave me alone?"

The Hairy Man answered, "If you give me your baby, I'll leave you alone."

Grandmammy opened the door, and there stood the Hairy Man. He was brown and HAIRY all over. [*Run a hand down each arm to indicate HAIRY.*] He had big red eyes [*With your hands, circle your eyes.*] and big yellow teeth. [*Bare your teeth.*] Worst of all, he dripped and drooled, and spit when he spoke. [*This has a rhythmic pattern.*] He was carrying a big, burlap sack. [*Hold one arm out to the side, creating a circle. Point to it with the other hand.*]

Grandmammy pointed to the small bed, where a little bundle lay. The Hairy Man ran to the bed, picked up the bundle, and stuffed it into his sack. "Just like that, jump into my sack!" [*Hold one arm out to the side, creating a circle. Point to it with the other hand.*] Then he turned around and grinned, showing his big yellow teeth. [*Bare your teeth.*] The Hairy Man said, [*pause*] "Booga, wooga, wooga, shim bim bam, I am the Hairy Man, YES . . . I . . . AM!" [*Pause after "Yes," "I," and "Am," emphasizing the power of the Hairy Man.*]

Grandmammy told Wiley to come out of hiding, and they watched the Hairy Man run across the yard. He stopped and opened the sack. Imagine his surprise when a small, baby pig bounced out of that bundle!

The Hairy Man yelled, "Yoooou fooooooled meeeee!" [*Draw out the vowels in each word.*]

Grandmammy replied, "I said you could have my baby but I didn't say what KIND of baby you could have, and that's my baby PIG!"

The Hairy Man was so mad he went screaming off into the swamps, pulling out his hair. Since Grandmammy and Wiley fooled the Hairy Man three times, he never bothered them again. You see, Grandmammy was from the swamps. She was real smart, and she knew magic. And Grandmammy and Wiley lived a loooooooong, happy life.

Notes on Story Sources

"A Dark, Dark Story" was adapted from "In a Dark, Dark Room," in *In A Dark, Dark Room,* by Alvin Schwartz (New York: HarperTrophy, 1984); and "In a Dark, Dark Wood," in *Haunts & Taunts,* by Jean Chapman (London: Award Publications, 1976).

"The Attic" was adapted from "The Attic," in *Scary Stories to Tell in the Dark,* by Alvin Schwartz (New York: HarperCollins, 1981); and "The Nail in the Attic," from the Boy Scout Trail Web site, www.boyscouttrail.com/content/story/nail_in_the_attic-992.asp.

"Blood Red Lips" was adapted from "Bony Fingers," in *The Scary Story Reader,* by Richard Young and Judy Dockery Young (Little Rock, AR: August House Publishers, 1993).

"Bloody Finger" was adapted from "The Ghost with the Bloody Fingers," in *Scary Stories to Tell in the Dark,* by Alvin Schwartz (New York: HarperCollins, 1981); and "Bloody Fingers," in *Scared Silly: Stories to Make You Gasp and Giggle,* by Judith Bauer Stamper (New York: Scholastic, 2004).

"The Coffin" was adapted from "Stop the Coffin," in *Favorite Scary Stories of American Children,* by Richard Young and Judy Dockery Young (Little Rock, AR: August House, 1990); "Stop That Coffin!" in *Scared Silly: Stories to Make You Gasp and Giggle,* by Judith Bauer Stamper (New York: Scholastic, 2004); and a fantastic version I heard from a teller at the Ocean Springs Storytelling Festival in Ocean Springs, Mississippi, in 1996. Since then, my version of "The Coffin" has taken on a life of its own.

"The Ghost of Mable Gable" was adapted from my memories of the story as a young girl, when I was in the Girl Scouts. It's a classic "shaggy dog" campfire tale. It was funny then, and it's even funnier now!

"Going on a Ghost Hunt" was adapted from the traditional story "Going on a Bear Hunt."

"The Golden Arm" was adapted from "The Golden Arm," in *Spooky Stories for a Dark & Stormy Night,* by Alice Low (New York: Hyperion Books for Children, 1994); and "The Golden Arm," in *Even More Short & Shivery* by Robert D. San Souci (New York: Scholastic, 1987).

"The Graveyard Dare" was adapted from "The Girl Who Stood on a Grave," in *Scary Stories to Tell in the Dark,* by Alvin Schwartz (New York: HarperCollins, 1981).

"The Great Big Hairy Toe" was adapted from "The Hairy Toe," in *Haunts & Taunts,* by Jean Chapman (London: Award Publications, 1976); "The Big Toe," in *Scary Stories to Tell in the Dark,* by Alvin Schwartz (New York: HarperCollins, 1981); "The Hairy Toe," in *Scared Silly: Stories to Make You Gasp and Giggle,* by Judith Bauer Stamper (New York: Scholastic, 2004); and "The Big Hairy Toe," in *Jackie Tales,* by Jackie Torrence (New York: Avon Books, 1998).

"The Green, Green Ribbon" was adapted from "The Green Ribbon," in *In A Dark, Dark Room,* by Alvin Schwartz (New York: HarperTrophy, 1984); and "The Yellow Ribbon," in *Jackie Tales* by Jackie Torrence (New York: Avon Books, 1998).

"The Gunny Wolf" was adapted from "The Gunny Wolf," in *A Treasury of American Folklore,* edited by B.A. Botkin (New York: Crown, 1944); and *The Gunniwolf,* retold by Wilhelmina Harper (New York: Dutton Children's Books, 2003; original text, 1918 by Wilhelmina Harper).

"The Hitchhiker" was adapted from "The Vanishing Hitchhiker," in *The Vanishing Hitchhiker,* by Jan Harold Brunvand (New York: W.W. Norton, 1981); and "The Bus Stop," in *Scary Stories 3: More Tales to Chill Your Bones,* by Alvin Schwartz (New York: HarperCollins, 1991).

"I Know an Old Lady Who Swallowed a Cat" is an original adaptation of the traditional story, "I Know an Old Lady Who Swallowed a Fly."

"Rap, Rap, Rap!" was adapted from "Rap! Rap! Rap!" in *Spooky Stories for a Dark & Stormy Night,* by Alice Low (New York: Hyperion Books for Children, 1994); "Rap, Rap, Rap!" in *Scared Silly: Stories to Make You Gasp and Giggle,* by Judith Bauer Stamper (New York: Scholastic, 2004); and "Rap . . .Rap . . . Rap!" in *Favorite Scary Stories of American Children,* by Richard Young and Judy Dockery Young (Little Rock, AR: August House, 1990).

"Raw Head and Bloody Bones" was adapted from "Old Raw Head," in *Favorite Scary Stories of American Children,* by Richard Young and Judy Dockery Young (Little Rock, AR: August House, 1990); "Old Raw Head," in *Even More Short & Shivery,* by Robert D. San Souci (New York: Scholastic, 1998); and "Raw Head and Bloody Bones," in *Whistle in the Graveyard: Folktales to Chill Your Bones,* by Maria Leach (New York: Viking Press, 1974).

"The Strange Visitor" was adapted from "The Strange Visitor," in *Spooky Stories for a Dark & Stormy Night,* by Alice Low (New York: Hyperion Books for Children, 1994); "The Strange Visitor," in *Scared Silly: Stories to Make You Gasp and Giggle,* by Judith Bauer Stamper (New York: Scholastic, 2004); and "What Do You Come For?" in *Scary Stories to Tell in the Dark,* by Alvin Schwartz (New York: HarperCollins, 1981).

"Taily Po" was adapted from "Taily-Po," in *The Scary Book,* by Joanna Cole and Stephanie Calmenson (New York: Beech Tree Edition, 1994); and "Tailypo," in *Short & Shivery,* by Robert D. San Souci (New York: Delacorte Press, 1987).

"The Teeny-Tiny Woman" was adapted from "Teeny-Tiny," in *English Fairy Tales,* by Joseph Jacobs (New York: Alfred A. Knopf, 1890).

"Tilly and the Heebie-Jeebie Man" was adapted from "I'm Coming Up the Stairs," in *Spooky Stories for a Dark & Stormy Night,* by Alice Low (New York: Hyperion Books for Children, 1994); and "Tillie Williams," in *The Scary Story Reader,* by Richard Young and Judy Dockery Young (Little Rock, AR: August House, 1993).

"The Viper" was adapted from "The Viper Is Coming," in *The Scary Book,* by Joanna Cole and Stephanie Calmenson (New York: Beech Tree Edition, 1994); "The Viper," in *The Scary Story Reader,* by Richard Young and Judy Dockery Young (Little Rock, AR: August House, 1993); and "The Viper," in *Scary Stories to Tell in the Dark,* by Alvin Schwartz (New York: HarperCollins, 1981).

"Wait Till Bubba Comes" was adapted from "Wait Till Martin Comes," in *Spooky Stories for a Dark & Stormy Night,* by Alice Low (New York: Hyperion Books for Children, 1994); "Wait Till Martin Comes," in *The Scary Book,* by Joanna Cole and Stephanie Calmenson (New York: Beech Tree Edition, 1994); and "Wait Till Martin Comes," in *Scary Stories to Tell in the Dark,* by Alvin Schwartz (New York: HarperCollins, 1981).

"Who Took My Money?" was adapted from "Clinkity Clink," in *More Scary Stories to Tell in the Dark,* by Alvin Schwartz (New York: HarperCollins, 1984).

"Who Will Keep Me Company?" was adapted from childhood memories of the story.

"Wiley and the Hairy Man" was adapted from "Wiley and the Hairy Man," in *Spooky Stories for a Dark & Stormy Night,* by Alice Low (New York: Hyperion Books for Children, 1994); and "The Hairy Man," in *Jackie Tales,* by Jackie Torrence (New York: Avon Books, 1998).

Web Resources

These are great Web resources for spooky stories!

American Folklore.net

www.americanfolklore.net/spooky-stories.html

A treasure trove of stories. The site has a great section on scary stories from all over the United States.

Boy Scout Trail

www.boyscouttrail.com

A great site for Scouts! There are a number of spooky stories on the site. I love the search feature you can use to find a scary story.

Campfire Stories

www.ultimatecampresource.com/site/camp-activities/campfire-stories.html

Want classic campfire stories? This site has them, and they are even categorized into "Legends," "Scary," and "Funny."

Scary Stories

www.scarystories.ca/

A wonderful site, filled with tons of scary stories from around the world.

Index

About the Author and Illustrator

Dianne de Las Casas is an author and award-winning storyteller who tours internationally presenting programs, educator/librarian training, workshops, and artist residencies. Her performances, dubbed "traditional folklore gone fun" and "revved-up storytelling," are full of energetic audience participation. Dianne's professional books include *Story Fest: Crafting Story Theater Scripts*; *Kamishibai Story Theater: The Art of Picture Telling*; *Handmade Tales: Stories to Make and Take*; *Tangram Tales: Story Theater Using the Ancient Chinese Puzzle*; *The Story Biz Handbook*; and *Scared Silly: 25 Tales to Tickle and Thrill*. Her children's books include *The Cajun Cornbread Boy*, *Madame Poulet & Monsieur Roach*, and *Mama's Bayou*. Visit her Web site at www.storyconnection.net.

Soleil Lisette is a graphic design student at Louisiana State University in Baton Rouge. Since she was two years old, she could always be found with a pen in her hand, drawing! Her career aspirations include illustrating children's books and beginning her own line of cosmetics. When not at school, Soleil lives in the New Orleans area. Visit Soleil's Web site at www.soleil-lisette.com.